GATSBY

DEATH OF AN IRISHMAN

GATSBY

DEATH OF AN IRISHMAN

*F. Scott Fitzgerald and
his search for identity*

PATRICK O'SULLIVAN GREENE

EASTWOOD BOOKS

First published in 2025 by Eastwood Books

Dublin, Ireland
www.eastwoodbooks.com
www.wordwellbooks.com

First edition

Eastwood Books is an imprint of the Wordwell Group

Eastwood Books
The Wordwell Group
Unit 9, 78 Furze Road
Sandyford
Dublin, Ireland

The Wordwell Group is a member of Publishing Ireland, the Irish
Book Publishers' Association.

ISBN: 978-1-916742-65-9 (Paperback)
ISBN: 978-1-916742-75-8 (ePub)

British Library Cataloguing in Publication Data.
A catalogue record for this book is available from the National
Library of Ireland and the British Library.

Copyediting by Heidi Houlihan
Layout and design by Wordwell
Printed in Ireland by Sprint Books

To my mother, Maureen

TABLE OF CONTENTS

Acknowledgements

Many thanks to Ronan McGreevy, *Irish Times* journalist and author, and Ronan Colgan, Group Managing Director of the Wordwell Group; they have provided ongoing encouragement and support. Thanks also to Heidi Houlihan for copy editing and everyone at Wordwell for their work in transforming a raw manuscript into a published book.

I was fortunate to have the wonderful support of the Celtic Junction Arts Center in Saint Paul, Minnesota, the birth place of F. Scott Fitzgerald. Thank you to the Saint Paul Public Library, the American Irish Historical Society in New York and The Princess Grace Irish Library in Monaco, as well as Patrice Buckley for her tour of Long Island.

Thanks to the staff of Kerry Library for their courtesy and efficiency, and to professional archivists everywhere who perform an invaluable task. My appreciation also goes to the staff of Lir and Noelle's where much of this book was written, fuelled by expresso and hot chocolate.

Thanks to family and friends at home and abroad.

QUOTATIONS

'"Go on, my child."

"Of – of not believing I was the son of my parents."

"What?" The interrogation was distinctly startled.

"Of not believing that I was the son of my parents."

"Why not?"

"Oh, just pride," answered the penitent airily.

"You mean you thought you were too good to be the son of your parents?"

"Yes, Father."'

F. Scott Fitzgerald, 'Absolution'

'Amory Blaine suspected that being Irish was being somewhat common.'

F. Scott Fitzgerald, This Side of Paradise

'He looked – and this is said in all contempt for the babbled slander of his garden – as if he had "killed a man." For a moment the set of his face could be described in just that fantastic way.'

F. Scott Fitzgerald, The Great Gatsby

'Because of our Irish blood, we are handicapped in America and consequently, have an interest in the freedom of the race.'

Judge Daniel F. Cohalan

PROLOGUE

North and South

Twenty-five years after General Lee surrendered to Ulysses S. Grant at Appomattox, Edward Fitzgerald of Maryland entered a matrimonial union with Mollie McQuillan of Minnesota, setting in motion a civil war of a different kind.

Mollie's father, Philip F. McQuillan, left Fermanagh as a child with his parents in the early 1840s. The family settled in Galena, a large steamboat hub on the Mississippi river in the midwestern state of Illinois. In 1857, swept up in the pioneering spirit, he steamed upriver to St Paul, Minnesota, the last navigable point on the Mississippi; the kind of place an ambitious twenty-three-year-old could make his fortune. Beyond lay untamed frontier territory.

McQuillan began his career in St Paul keeping the accounts for Temple & Beaupre, an up-and-coming grocery wholesale business.[1] There was opportunity in food supply in the rapidly expanding frontier town. St Paul had grown from barely 1,000 people at the beginning of the decade to over 10,000 people by 1860; it would double over each of the next two decades. With sufficient experience of the trade obtained and a little capital saved, McQuillan made an entrepreneurial leap by opening a small grocery store two years after arriving. Expanding into wholesale in 1862, he prospered through the civil war and during the opening of the Midwest territories. Ten years later, P.F. McQuillan & Co. was operating out of a four-storey building.[2]

A report went around in July 1875 that the renamed Beaupre & Kelly, his former employer, was buying him out due to ill health. McQuillan quickly dismissed the report calling the founder of the rumour a 'villain'.[3] In a surprise move the following month, Bruno Beaupre retired from Beaupre & Kelly, took an interest in his former employee's business, and together they formed McQuillan Beaupre & Co. The transition made the new company 'the most popular one in the State'. The new partner was delighted to be associated 'with a conservative firm after his own liking'.[4]

McQuillan saw further opportunity in the expansion of the railroad. He was elected to the board of directors of the Western Railroad Company of Minnesota in 1877, along with James J. Hill, who had arrived in St Paul at the same time and had spent a year with Temple & Beaupre.[5] Hill had built a successful steamboat and fuel business and was determined to participate in the unprecedented opportunity presented by building and operating railroads.

As well as expanding his business interests, McQuillan built a family life. He married Louisa Allen, the daughter of Catherine Mahoney and Joseph Allen, an Irish emigrant carpenter and building contractor from Laois.[6]

Philip and Louisa had eight children, with Mollie, the eldest, born in August 1859.[7] Home for the respected family was an elegant three-storey Victorian house. Mollie led a privileged life, receiving her education in New York and enjoying shopping trips to Paris.

The earlier reports of Philip's ill health may have had some foundation as he died at home on 11 April 1877 from Bright's disease, inflammation of the kidneys.[8] He had just turned forty-three. It was an untimely death for a man thriving on his initial business success and about to participate in the expansion of the railroad into the remaining frontier territories of Minnesota, the Dakotas and Montana. Philip left behind a business transacting 'millions of dollars annually.'[9] The *Chicago Tribune* described him as 'an unusually successful merchant, and in every respect worthy of the high esteem in which he has been held by all acquaintances.'[10] Local newspapers in St Paul generously appraised his life.

> He came here a poor boy with but a few dollars in his pocket, depending solely on a clear head, sound judgment, good habits, strict honesty and willing hands, with strict integrity his guiding motive. How these qualities have aided him is shown in the immense business he has built up, the acquisition of large property outside, and the universal respect felt for him by the businessmen of the county, among whom probably no man was better known or stood higher.[11]

Louisa McQuillan, drawing on all her strength and with the benefit of a substantial inheritance, ensured seventeen-year-old Mollie and her four surviving siblings continued to live an upper-middle-class lifestyle, including expensive vacations. The *Saint Paul Globe* reported in 1888 that 'Mrs. McQuillan and family will soon depart for Europe.'[12]

Seven years before Philip McQuillan arrived in St Paul to begin his conquest of the American Midwest, Michael Fitzgerald married Cecilia Ashton Scott in 1850 in Baltimore, Maryland. Fitzgerald was forty-five, the son of an Irish emigrant father. She was eighteen, the daughter of John Scott and Elizabeth Key, whose family roots traced back to the first Maryland families in the seventeenth-century. They had Catholicism in common. Proud of their southern breeding, though without a large fortune, the Ashton Scott's lineage included Francis Scott Key, the author of the 'Star-Spangled Banner'.

Edward Fitzgerald was born to Michael and Cecilia in 1853. As a boy, he proudly rowed Confederate spies across a river during the civil war.[13] His cousin Mary Surratt was hanged for her role in the assassination of President Lincoln; John Wilkes Booth had planned the killing in her boarding house. After his father's death when he was just two years old, Edward was raised a dapper, well-mannered southern gentleman. However, as soon as he could, he left the South to get as far away from the scenes of the civil war as possible and seek his fortune in the North.[14]

Small in stature, genteel in nature and lacking force of character, Edward settled in ambitious St Paul. He went into the wicker furniture business, a sector controlled nationally by two fiercely competitive companies. It was there that he met Mollie McQuillan. They married in 1890 in Washington where Mollie's mother had a house, with the governor of Minnesota attending the wedding.

So commenced the familial civil war between the mercantile McQuillans looking down upon the poorer southern Fitzgeralds, who paraded their breeding and affectations before the famine-Irish northerners. Francis Scott Key Fitzgerald, born to Edward and Mollie in 1896, recalled growing-up in an atmosphere of 'crack, wise crack and countercrack', with each family imposing their 'usual exaggerated ancestral pretensions'.[15]

PART 1

THIS SIDE OF PARADISE

Blood of Some Potentiality

Edward and Mollie married late in life by the standards of the time, at thirty-seven and thirty years respectively. They were blessed with a daughter in 1892, named Louisa after Mollie's mother. Baby Mary Ashton was born in 1894. Then just two years later, in 1896 a pandemic struck St Paul when Mollie was pregnant with her next child, Scott. Louisa and Mary Ashton were taken. Scott was born within months of the loss of his two little sisters. Four years later Mollie gave birth to another girl who lived for just one hour. Scott's sole surviving sibling, Annabel, was born in Syracuse, New York in 1901.

Annabel's birth in Syracuse, rather than St Paul, stemmed from another family crisis. Edward's business, the American Rattan and Willow Works, collapsed in 1898, forcing him to uproot the family from St Paul to take a job as a soap salesman with Procter & Gamble, first in Buffalo, then Syracuse, then back in Buffalo. In 1908, the fifty-five-year-old was let go. The experience haunted his young son. In fear of poverty, Scott prayed, 'Dear God, please don't let us go to the poorhouse'.[16]

Edward had received one too many blows in life; the death and destruction of the civil war, the loss of three daughters, the collapse of his business and the indignity of losing his job. Scott witnessed a change in him: 'That morning he had gone out a comparatively young man, a man full of strength, full of confidence. He came home that evening, an old man, a completely broken man. He had lost his essential drive, his immaculateness of purpose. He was a failure the rest of his days.'[17]

Edward transplanted the family back to St Paul and in near penury they temporarily moved into Mollie's mother's house. A brother-in-law provided a desk in an office from where Edward eked out a meagre living as a small wholesale grocery salesman. Clinging to the remnants of their former middle-class lifestyle with the support of McQuillan financial subventions, they moved frequently between rented accommodation in the affluent Summit Avenue neighbourhood. Edward learned to live with Mollie's persistent refrain to Scott, 'If it weren't for your Grandfather McQuillan, where would we be now?'

Being Irish and Catholic marked Scott as different to his predominantly Anglo-Protestant friends on Summit Avenue. He once remarked that they thought Catholics secretly drilled in their churches to overthrow the government.[18] However, he encountered little serious ethnic or religious bias in St Paul. French-Canadian fur traders and settlers, mainly Catholic, were the first to take advantage of the establishment of Fort Snelling at the confluence of the Mississippi and Minnesota rivers. Inevitably, missionaries followed in their wake and Catholicism prospered with the arrival of German, Irish and Scottish immigrants. One year before Scott returned from the east, the community demonstrated its power and ambition by laying the foundation stone for the domed Cathedral of Saint Paul which towers over the city from the top of Summit Hill.

Being Irish classed Scott as merely common. Always conscious of his position in society, he later delineated the social stratification of the St Paul of his youth, a 'three-generation' town that gave it a sense of superiority over more recently established urban centres. At the top were the families whose grandparents came from the East with a little money and culture; then came the descendants of the big self-made merchants, the old settlers of the sixties and seventies, including the McQuillans. These were stratified further as American-English-Scotch, or German or Irish, 'looking down upon each other somewhat in the order named'. The Irish condescension lay less in religious difference than in a sense of a 'taint of political corruption in the East'.[19] Refusing any classification were two or three nationally known and enormously rich families.

Determined to endow her son with the life advantages, expectations and privileges she enjoyed as a child, Mollie sent Scott to the non-denominational St Paul Academy and paid for dance lessons. Her husband turned out a disappointing failure, but his southern family provided Scott a lineage that stretched further back than many of the old families of St Paul. Mollie took unique pride in the family connection to Francis Scott Key, and liked to talk about it.[20] Proudly naming her son for his ancestor, not for his father or either grandfather, she and Scott liked to claim him as his great granduncle, though he was a second cousin, three times removed.[21]

Mollie indulged and spoiled Scott and provided little in the way of discipline. Edward did his best as a moral guide, but added southern pretensions to an inflated ego. The teenage boy believed the world revolved around him.[22] After returning to St Paul and quickly earning a reputation as the 'freshest' boy in school, a fellow student wrote a letter to the school paper, 'Will someone poison Scotty or find some means to shut his mouth.'[23]

He attended parties for his friends on Summit Avenue in Victorian mansions known by their family name and played on streets named for successful parents and grand-parents. He went to bobsleigh parties at the Town and Country Club. During warm summer months, when the elite retreated to their vacation homes on the shoreline of White Bear Lake, about nine miles north of St Paul he had to ride the electric streetcar out to the exclusive White Bear Yacht Club to meet his friends and play tennis, swim and sail.

The most imposing mansion on Summit Avenue was the home of James J. Hill, who deservedly bore the soubriquet 'Empire Builder' for his exploits in the rail business. Not only had he the entrepreneurial vision to explore and colonise the frontier territories, he had the necessary daring, endurance and persistence of a pioneer; travelling by stagecoach and horseback over poor roads and across flooded streams, through raging snow storms, and falling through iced rivers and fending off thieves and wolves, and witnessing first-hand the ill-fated Fenian invasion of Canada. Complementing strong features and a powerful frame, he had the intelligence, hands-on work ethic and attention to detail to take his railroad across the continent to the Pacific Ocean.

Like the Cathedral of St Paul, across from which it stood, Hill's home projected power and achievement. When completed in 1891, the Romanesque mansion was the largest in the state extending over five floors boasting thirteen bathrooms, twenty-two fireplaces and a two-storey skylit art gallery, and when Scott saw it for the first time, electric lighting.[24] Hill married Mary Mehegan, a waitress in the dining room of the Merchants Hotel in St Paul and the daughter of Irish Catholic immigrants. He financed three years at a finishing school in preparation for her new life, which included raising ten children. Though Hill was of Scotch-Irish Protestant heritage, the children were raised Catholic and he built and endowed a Catholic Seminary.

Scott's Aunt, Annabel McQuillan, was maid of honour at the wedding of Hill's daughter Mary in 1888. He grew up with the Hill grandchildren, five of whom would have their own homes on Summit Avenue.[25] He must have pondered what his life would have been like if his grandfather had not died before the railway boom.

Mollie's social expectations for her son came back to haunt her. Becoming ashamed of his Irish roots, he would refer to the McQuillans as 'straight 1850 potato famine Irish'. Her appearance and eccentric behaviour embarrassed him. Rather plain and dowdy with unkempt hair and a careless dresser, Mollie appeared 'witchlike' to his friends.[26] They saw her breaking in new shoes one at a time; she had a manicure on her right hand only because she could do the left herself; she was known to make embarrassingly inappropriate comments. 'I'm trying to decide,' she said to a woman whose husband was ill, 'how you'll look in mourning.'[27]

Envious of the successful fathers and elegant mothers of his mainly Anglo-friends, the young Scott used his imagination to escape and reject his parents and his common Irish heritage. As a nine-year-old he fantasised that he was a foundling of royal lineage left wrapped in a blanket on the family doorstep.[28] For a time, he imagined himself the 'son of a king, a king who ruled the whole world'.[29] As a thirteen-year-old manoeuvring for his first kiss, as he later wrote, he posed as 'awful good-looking and *English* [his italics], sort of'.[30]

Though humiliated by his father's business failure, Scott distanced himself from his Irish roots by embracing his southern lineage, and not just the Ashton Scott Key line. With subtle reinvention, he denied that he was Irish on both sides, claiming the Fitzgeralds as both Norman and colonial American. Scott adopted Edward's southern courtesy and manners. On Sunday mornings, he proudly went down town with his father to have their shoes shined and buy the newspapers.[31] Inspired by his father's stories of the civil war, he developed an early sentimental attachment to the lost cause of the Confederacy. In the story, 'A Debt of Honor', written by Scott for the St Paul Academy magazine, a Confederate soldier falls asleep on sentry duty and is pardoned by General Lee. He redeems himself by an act of heroism and is killed at the Battle of Chancellorsville.

Scott sought familial pride in the blood connection to Francis Scott Key. In a later short story, 'May Day', an ill-nourished demobilised soldier named Carrol *Key* possesses a name 'hinting that in his veins, however thinly diluted by generations of degeneration, ran blood of some potentiality'.

CELTIC SEED

Mollie sent Scott eastward to the Catholic Newman preparatory school in Lakewood, New Jersey in the autumn of 1911. Funded by grandmother McQuillan, the change was thought necessary to improve the grades of a boy absorbed in extracurricular activities and writing.

For Scott, aged fifteen, the move offered 'infinite possibilities', but he experienced the same transition issues he had at the St Paul Academy on his return from the east.[32] He was unpopular, bossy and boastful. He was ashamed of being, as he later wrote, 'one of the poorest boys in a rich boys' school'.[33] Friendless, miserable and homesick, he found solace in the electric lights of New York – the forest fire of Broadway – and beautiful girls that were easily accessible by train. After seeing Ina Claire in *The Quaker Girl* and Gertrude Bryan in *Little Boy Blue*, he fell in 'hopeless and melancholy' love.[34]

Determined to make a fresh start following the Christmas vacation, he sought prominence in writing and made friends with Charles 'Sap' Donahoe, another westerner from Seattle, a popular student, good scholar and fine athlete.[35] Travelling home together on long memorable train journeys cemented their relationship and Scott maintained a lifelong respect for his new friend. Donahoe understood him. 'He was unpopular starting out,' he recalled of their time at Newman, 'partly because his good looks promoted classification as a sissy which was reinforced by a lack of physical courage. But he had an insight into character and motive which enabled him to more than hold his own in worldly disputes, and finally, by practice I suppose, he became inured to psychological impacts with either the school authorities or the more important of his fellow students which in time won him a sense of belonging where his talents had some acclaim.'[36]

Academic achievement was not a priority. He spent much of his first year at Newman attempting to write a play, working on a libretto, playing baseball, doing athletics and travelling frequently to New York. Grandmother and Aunt Annabel visited the school in February 1912 and he travelled south to Norfolk to call on his favourite cousin Cecila 'Ceci' Taylor the following month. Scott had been a ribbon-bearer at her wedding. Now widowed, Ceci had four young girls and struggled financially. He brought the kids presents. He passed only four of his summer examinations.

On the train ride back west to St Paul, he wrote a full-length play, *Captured Shadow*, a crime comedy. The Elizabethan Dramatic Club, a group he organised, performed the play before an audience of several hundred. He played the role of a gentleman burglar who was not really a thief and the performance generated sixty dollars for a local charity.

With White Bear Yacht Club continuing to be the summer social hub, Scott noted with teenage frustration, 'Began to feel lack of automobile.'[37] A dance at White Bear that summer left an enduring scar. The evening began with him begging a ride out from St Paul with some boys who did not want him along, and ended with him left out of a party organised right under his nose.[38] Reflecting on this period he wrote the short story, 'Winter Dreams'. A Midwest boy, the son of the owner of the second-best grocery store in town, aspires to be part of the old-money elite. Working part-time as a caddie at the Black Bear golf club, he quits when disrespected by a spoiled rich girl.

Returning for his second academic year at Newman, Scott first encountered Father Sigourney Fay, a charismatic, erudite and ambitious priest from a prominent Philadelphia family. Fay toured all parts of the Catholic world, as Scott described, 'rather like an exiled Stuart king waiting to be called to the rule of his land'.[39] The sixteen-year-old boy and the thirty-seven-year-old priest struck up a paternal, mutually flattering and vanity-filled relationship. Writing about the unorthodox coupling, Scott described how the 'jovial, impressive prelate who could dazzle an embassy ball, and the green-eyed, intent youth, in his first long trousers, accepted in their own minds a relation of father and son within a half-hour's conversation'.[40]

Almost Albino, overweight and perfumed, the priest cut an unusual figure. An Episcopalian convert, he served as an adviser to the influential Cardinal Gibbons of Baltimore and roamed comfortably in high literary and social circles. He taught liturgy and Ecclesiastical Greek at Catholic University in Washington, DC, and had been appointed a director of the Newman school.[41]

Fay recognised in Scott a precocious young talent whom he hoped to nurture into a future great Catholic writer. Scott, in turn, saw an opportunity to broaden his intellectual horizon beyond the confines and limitations of his parents and the middle west. In March 1913, Fay invited him to his home in Washington, bringing him into his wide social circle and introducing him to wine and cigarettes. When Scott returned to Newman, he had his first taste of whiskey and was 'Tight at Susquehanna' the following month.[42]

In Scott's dramatised account of his first meeting with Fay, they immediately established their mutual loathing of all science and mathematics, their love of English and history and their critical views of Harvard, Princeton and Yale before they 'slipped briskly into an intimacy from which they never recovered'.[43] Scott related his admiration for historical underdogs, including Charles Stuart, the eighteenth-century claimant to the thrones of England, Scotland and Ireland.

'I was for Bonnie Prince Charlie'

'Of course you were – and for Hannibal –'

'Yes, and for the Southern Confederacy.'

Scott shocked Father Fay with the revelation of an underdog cause that he could not support and his very personal reason, declaring that he was 'rather sceptical about being an Irish patriot − he suspected that being Irish was being somewhat common'. Fay reassured him on both counts: 'Ireland was a romantic lost cause and Irish people quite charming, and that it should, by all means, be one of his principal biases.'

Fay introduced Scott to Shane Leslie, an urbane twenty-seven-year-old author and poet, whom he described as the 'most romantic figure I had ever known'.[44] Sir John Leslie, 3rd Baronet, adopted the name Shane, an anglicised Irish version of his first name, and converted to Catholicism against his parents' wishes, renouncing his right of succession to a vast family estate, though retaining his title. Educated at Eton and Cambridge, he was a first cousin to the young Winston Churchill − their mothers were two of the prominent American Jerome sisters. Leslie captivated Scott with tales of meeting Tolstoy in Russia and swimming with Rupert Brooke, the idealistic English poet.[45] In short, Leslie represented everything to which Scott aspired.

Ironically, and with unintended insight, Scott viewed Leslie as 'a young Englishman of the governing classes when the sense of being one must have been ... like the sense of being a Roman citizen'.[46] As a proud Irishman of Anglo-Protestant heritage, Leslie would have protested. However, he did see himself as part of a governing class. A fervent believer in Home Rule as a solution to the Irish question, he advocated for a parliament in Dublin attending to domestic affairs, with Ireland remaining loyal to the King and continuing as part of the British Empire.

Through his two new mentors, Scott experienced Eastern elitism and upper-class Catholic cosmopolitanism for the first time. He did not regard them as his inferiors, as he perceived his parents and teachers to be, and they made Catholicism appear 'a dazzling, golden thing' in stark contrast to the scowling priests of the midwestern church.[47] They also planted a seed of interest in his Celtic roots that would take time to germinate.

His intellectual horizon broadened when Fay introduced him to Henry Adams, a prominent historian and journalist, and a descendent of two presidents.[48] No doubt Scott communicated his familial connection to Francis Scott Key. Over a memorable lunch, later put in dramatic form, Adams educated Scott on three significant European political leaders: William Gladstone, former Prime Minister of the United Kingdom, Otto von Bismarck, former Chancellor of the German Empire and Charles Stewart Parnell, the statesman known as the 'Uncrowned King of Ireland'. All died within a three-year span between 1888 and 1891; Gladstone and Bismark were in their eighties and Parnell was just forty-five.

Charles Stewart Parnell had been leader of the Irish Home Rule movement until his naming in divorce proceedings drew the ire of the Catholic church, ending his political career. The son of Anglo-Irish landowner John Henry Parnell and Delia Tudor Stewart, the daughter of

American naval hero Admiral Charles Stewart, he was elected to the House of Commons in 1875 and became president of the Irish National Land League in 1879. Combining parliamentary methods with civil agitation in pursuit of fair rent, fixity of tenure and freedom to sell for impoverished Irish farmers, he was imprisoned for seven months.

During a four-month tour of North America in 1880, Parnell addressed the House of Representatives and spoke in sixty-two cities across the United States and Canada. In St Paul, where his speech raised $1,700, he met the influential Bishop Ireland who canvassed his support for the *Catholic Colonisation Bureau*, his programme to relocate families from Connemara to western Minnesota. Parnell believed land reform rather than emigration was the best solution for Ireland.[49]

He forged a unique political alliance, known as the New Departure, with John Devoy, the outstanding leader of the underground Irish republican movement, Clan-na-Gael. 'Amiable to meet, vitriolic of pen,' wrote Shane Leslie of Devoy, '… the last of the real Fenians.'[50] This was an accurate assessment only to a point. The old Fenian also spoke French, a legacy from his time in the Foreign Legion, and he had a little Spanish; he was a voracious reader and a keen geopolitical analyst. His gift for language, peppered with cultural and political references, shone in weekly editorials in the *Gaelic American*, the newspaper he founded in 1903.

Arrested in Ireland in 1866, he spent five hungry, rock-breaking years in English prisons before being exiled to America. An innovative and visionary revolutionary, he used his intelligence and management skills to continue the republican fight from the slums of New York City. He organised the rescue of six prisoners from an English penal colony in Australia – a logistical marvel that extended over two years and 12,000 miles, ending with the rescue ship, *Catalpa*, triumphantly entering New York harbour in 1876. Shortly after, he funded young Irish inventor John Holland to develop a submarine, seeing the potential to threaten English warships. A later prototype, combining electric motors for submerged travel and gasoline engines, was purchased by the US navy.

Parnell and Devoy split in 1882 when the Home Rule leader reverted to purely constitutional means to achieve his political aims. However, their close relationship nearly toppled him a few years later, when journalist Richard Piggott forged letters in his handwriting appearing to condone the 'Phoenix Park Murders', the 1882 fatal stabbing of the chief secretary and under-secretary of the English administration in Ireland. In what became known as the Piggott Forgeries affair, *The Times* of London eagerly published the letters in an attempt to discredit Parnell, forcing the British government to set up a parliamentary inquiry. Meanwhile, Devoy had fallen victim to a talented English spy, Henri Le Caron, a French-Canadian physician with an Irish mother and a veteran of the Fenian invasion of Canada. Under his real name, Thomas Beech, he made a surprise appearance as a key witness at the inquiry, which finally exonerated Parnell when the letters were revealed as forgeries.[51]

Scott neglected academic work again during his second year at Newman. A fellow student commented that he received poor grades because he read so many books.[52] Finding his time at the school profitless, he set his sights on Princeton but failed to meet the admission standard in the entrance examination, even with some minor cheating ('cribbing').[53] Returning to St Paul for the summer, he became increasingly conscious of his wealth disparity, noting with teenage envy, 'Automobile question grows worse.'[54] The Elizabethan Dramatic Club put on another of his plays, *The Coward*, a drama centred on a young Confederate soldier who redeemed himself through an act of bravery.[55] Following a sold-out show, the play was performed for a second time at the White Bear Yacht Club.

Scott was admitted to Princeton in September 1913 after taking make-up examinations during the summer vacation.

Spires and Gargoyles

Scott chose Presbyterian Princeton, one of nine colonial colleges chartered before the revolution, because it was preferred by southern gentlemen, a pose he chose to adopt. Romanticising the college as 'lazy and good-looking and aristocratic', he could disconnect from the middle west and his McQuillan roots.[56]

Almost destined for priest-ridden Georgetown, when Aunt Annabel offered to fund his education on condition it be Catholic, Grandmother McQuillan's death in June 1913 saved him from the ignominy. Mollie's inheritance was sufficient to send her son to Princeton. He was embarrassed by the source of his Ivy-League funding. In an autobiographical account of his Princeton years, his alter-ego protagonist admires a fellow student as 'a perfect type of aristocrat … the eternal example of what the upper class tries to be'. But he experiences a 'curious sinking sensation' when told the shocking truth that the student's father was 'a grocery clerk who made a fortune in Tacoma real estate'.[57]

Riveted by the hierarchical social system at Princeton, controlled by students from the more prestigious preparatory schools, he felt like an outsider inside the hallowed campus, observing the freshmen from the elite feeder schools 'eating at certain tacitly reserved tables in Commons, dressing in their own corners of the gymnasium, and drawing unconsciously about them a barrier of the slightly less important but socially ambitious to protect them'.[58] An Irish Catholic from the Midwest prepped at Newman School ranked low in the social order. With a limited allowance compared to other students, he ate at a short-order diner offering a charge account and seclusion from curious upper-class eyes.

Notwithstanding his social position, Scott was determined to become one of the 'gods' of the class. 'Oh, it isn't that I mind the glittering caste system,' declares his alter-ego. 'I like having a bunch of hot cats on top, but gosh, ... I've got to be one of them.' He failed at football, the fastest route to deification at Princeton, leaving only the board of the *Daily Princetonian* newspaper or presidency of the influential musical comedy Triangle Club. He would also need to receive an invitation to join one of the prestigious university eating clubs in his sophomore year.

He befriended John Peale Bishop, a southerner from West Virginia. Bishop would gain recognition as a poet and man of letters and had been encouraged by his family to develop his literary talents, in contrast to Scott's experience. Christian Gauss, who taught French Romantic poetry at Princeton, one of the few teachers Scott admired, noted that even as a freshman Bishop 'had a self-possession and self-mastery which gave him the poise and bearing of a young English lord'.[59] Bishop served as a surrogate literary mentor to Scott, who quickly realised that some of his poetry professors 'really hated it and didn't know what it was about'.[60] He would later dismiss the English department at Princeton as 'top-heavy, undistinguished and with an uncanny knack for making literature distasteful to young men'.[61]

Scott also met his intellectual nemesis, the formidable Edmund 'Bunny' Wilson. The son of a brilliant trial lawyer and New Jersey attorney general, Wilson arrived from Hill, one of the elite preparatory schools. As a future highly regarded literary critic, Wilson adopted a smug and superior demeanour toward Scott, the only Catholic he met at Princeton.[62]

Although he failed some mid-year examinations, after Christmas vacation Scott devoted himself to writing the plot and seventeen song lyrics for the Triangle Club's elaborate musical production, setting the tone for his remaining time at Princeton. Father Fay visited in February and invited him to his mother's home at Deal Beach, New Jersey, following the June examinations. While maintaining his friendship with the priest, he just about clung to his Catholic faith in the face of college temptations, explaining to Bunny Wilson, 'Why I can go up to New York on a terrible party and then come back into the church and pray – and mean every word of it, too!'[63] After his stay at Deal Beach, he spent the remainder of the summer in St Paul, taking the lead role in another of his Elizabethan Drama Club productions.

On his return to Princeton in September and rooming at Patton Hall, he cut more classes to meet the challenge of completing and staging the Triangle Club production of his comedy, *Fie! Fie! Fi-Fi!* After failing a coordinate geometry examination, he was ruled ineligible to tour the play, which premiered on 19 December in Princeton before embarking on a successful 3,500-mile circuit.[64] Reviewers praised his script, one noting that 'F. S. Fitzgerald … could take his place right now with the brightest writers of witty lyrics in America'.[65]

His election as secretary of the Triangle Club made him a shoe-in for presidency in his senior year and he received bids from four eating clubs, choosing Cottage, one of the prestigious Big Four known for a large southern following.[66] On the night of the club elections, he wrestled in the snow with Sap Donahoe before passing out at the club dinner.[67] Scott increasingly played the clown and used alcohol to compensate for creeping insecurity.[68]

He spent Easter in Washington with Helen Walcott, a popular debutante, and her friend Ruth Sturtevant, a student at Farmington in Connecticut with whom he maintained a flirtatious correspondence.[69] To conclude an outstanding sophomore year before returning to St Paul for the summer, he was elected to the editorial board of the *Princeton Tiger*, the college humour magazine, and had his first stories published in the *Nassau Literary Review*.[70] However, he failed three of his seven courses.[71]

While his sophomore year at Princeton had been a triumph, his junior year unfolded as tragedy. Returning in September, he moved into Little Hall and flunked the retake exams. A college committee ruled him ineligible from holding campus office, ending his dream of becoming president of the Triangle Club, and prohibited him from touring *The Evil Eye*, the musical comedy that he and Bunny Wilson, now chairman of the *Nassau Lit*, had written together. Devastated at the loss of privilege, his dreams of deification were over.[72]

> To me college would never be the same. There were to be no badges of pride, no medals, after all … that night was the first time that I hunted down the spectre of womanhood that, for a little while, makes everything else seem unimportant … it was a harsh and bitter business to know that my career as a leader of men was over … Some old desire for personal dominance was broken and gone.[73]

Falling ill with what was thought to be malaria in November, though later diagnosed as tuberculosis under X-ray screening, he returned early to St Paul by train for Christmas. He recovered sufficiently to see the performance of *The Evil Eye* in his home town. According to Princeton records, Scott left the college permanently on 3 January 1916 due to 'scholastic deficiencies'. The authorities had taken the view that he used the excuse of illness to avoid taking his mid-year examinations. In May, he persuaded the reluctant dean to provide a letter stating that he had voluntarily withdrawn due to ill health and that he was fully at liberty to return.[74] The dean accompanied the letter with a sneering note, 'This is for your sensitive feelings. I hope you will find it soothing.'[75]

POOR BOYS, RICH GIRLS

Travelling back by train to St Paul through school and college for Christmas vacation was a special time for Scott. Those going further than Chicago gathered in the old Union Station to catch up with friends before taking the yellow railroad cars 'looking cheerful as Christmas itself' out into the winter night. During the holiday season of his sophomore year, Scott enjoyed catching up with Marie Hersey, an early crush and now platonic friend. They attended a dance together on Summit Avenue hosted by Louie Hill, one of the empire builders' offspring, whose home had a second-floor ballroom and a basement swimming pool.[76] When Marie invited her schoolfriend debutante Ginevra King to visit and he was introduced to her at a party at the Town and Country Club, he was determined to win her heart.

No ordinary debutante, the sixteen-year-old was the daughter of the extravagantly wealthy Chicago stockbroker, Charles Garfield King. Some might have considered winning her heart a quixotic challenge, but not Scott, who was on his way to becoming a Princeton deity at the time. Aware of his vulnerable points, he made full use of his compensating strengths. 'I didn't have the two top things – great animal magnetism or money,' he wrote. 'I had the two second things, tho', good looks and intelligence. So I always got the top girl.'[77] His lack of wealth and social standing did not appear to be a barrier for Ginevra. 'I'd marry any kind of a man under the sun,' she wrote to her new boyfriend in early 1915, '"Richman, poorman, beggarman, thief," etc., if I really loved him.'[78] She acknowledged that it was 'of course an outrageous thing to go completely against the wishes of your family'.

Cool, confident and distant, Ginevra was highly sought after, a quality Scott found thrilling in girls. She was more than a match for him. 'I know I am a flirt and I can't stop it,' she admitted after their first date at the movies. '… I am pretty good on the whole, but you know how much alike we are.'[79] The long-distance relationship blossomed through feverish love letters over the following months until they could meet again. In June he brought her to the Princeton prom, and afterwards they travelled to New York with a chaperone, where they dined at the Ritz, went to see *Nobody Home* at the Princess Theatre, a two-act play about a man seeking approval for the hand of a girl from her guardians. Then they partied at the Midnight Frolic cabaret.[80]

Stopping off at her home in Chicago on his way back to St Paul, Scott became jealous of Ginevra's friendship with other boys. A taunt made by Deering Davis, one of her polo-playing car-owning friends, irked the automobile-less Scott so much he noted it for posterity: 'I'm going to take Ginevra home in my electric [car].'[81] She had previously scolded Scott for suggesting that she was going to marry Davis, a future respected interior designer who would serve as an aviator during the war. The relationship between Scott and Ginevra appears to have been one-sided at times. 'No news from Ginevra,' he wrote of his despair in August during a visit to Sap Donahoe's family ranch in Montana, where he got drunk with cowboys and won $50 in poker.[82]

One of her letters inspired him to write a story entitled 'The Perfect Hour'. 'Someday – Scott – some day,' she wrote romantically. 'Perhaps in a year – two – three – We'll have that perfect hour! I want it – and so we'll have it!' They shared their thoughts on the romantic ideal for months. Ginevra penned her own satirical and tragic story on the search for the perfect hour. In it, a self-named heroine is trapped in a loveless marriage to an adulterous Russian noble; a reunion with a former lover, a movie producer named 'Fitz-Gerald', who made his fortune in the hope of winning her back, ends in failure.[83] His story, now lost, probably had a happier ending.

The relationship reached a turning point during the summer of 1916 when Scott was facing familiar problems back in St Paul: 'Car troubles … Hiding my college bills.'[84] On a visit to Ginevra's vacation home in Lake Forest, north of Chicago, a racially segregated protestant town off-limits to African-Americans and Jews, Scott found himself surrounded by Ginevra's tight social circle, the sons and daughters of the banking and business elite.

Irish, Catholic, middle-class boys were not common visitors. Once asked by a college friend what his father did, Scott lied that he worked as an engineer for James J. Hill; maybe he lied again to Ginevra's friends.[85] His distant family connection to Francis Scott Key offered little social capital and Confederate sympathisers were not welcome in solidly Yankee territory. Much later in life, he transcribed a dream that portrayed his insecurity among the elite of Lake Forest; he is living upstairs with his mother, on another floor are handsome, rich, young men, whom he knew slightly as a child and now wanted to know better, but they look at him suspiciously.

I talk to one who is agreeable and not at all snobbish, but obviously he does not encourage my acquaintance – whether because he considers me poor, unimportant, ill bred, or of ill renown I don't know, or rather don't think about – only I scent the polite indifference and even understand it. During this time I discover that there is a dance downstairs to which I am not invited. I feel that if they knew better how important I was, I should be invited.[86]

Although they enjoyed a 'petting party', other Ginevra suiters were present at Lake Forest that summer. Scott made a caustic note of 'beautiful Billy Mitchell', another polo player, a Harvard student and friend of Ginevra since childhood. He was the son of a bank president who happened to be a close friend of Charles Garfield King.[87] Scott had been jealous of her relationship with 'This

Mitchell' during their first month dating. 'I know one boy named Billy Mitchell,' she deflected casually. 'He is very nice, but don't think he likes me particularly well.'[88]

He faced a greater barrier in his romantic pursuit in her father. With charm and Anglo-Saxon features, Scott was an acceptable social caller on Ginevra at Lake Forest, but not as her future husband. In a loud voice meant to be overheard, Charles Garfield King dismissed his hopes declaring, 'poor boys shouldn't think of marrying rich girls'.[89]

Whether through filial rebellion, or genuine attraction, or just because she was a confident girl enjoying her teen-age years, Ginevra accepted his invitation to Princeton for the Yale game in November 1917. Two months later, however, she ended the relationship. His devastation went beyond the pain of lost first love. He had created an idealised version of Ginevra and romanticised their rela-tionship to literary heights. He now understood that good looks and intelligence counted for little in old money soci-ety. He could get the top girl, but not keep her.

Ginevra was more realistic about their teenage relation-ship. She enjoyed his company and found him very bright and witty, but she was never in love, later recalling, '… at this time I was definitely out for quantity not quality in beaux, and, although Scott was top man, I still wasn't serious enough not to want plenty of other attention! … Certainly my attitude didn't help an already super-sensi-tive and sentimental person.'[90] She remembered of their time together that he was 'always on the outside, looking in'.[91]

RISE OF THE CELT

Returning to Princeton in September 1916 to repeat his third year, a demoralising prospect, Scott roomed with Paul Dickey at Little Hall and almost 'flunked out' again after failing mid-year exams.[92] His story for the Triangle show was rejected, but he wrote the song lyrics to Dickey's music. During the spring months he appeared thirteen times in the *Nassau Lit*, with a play, four stories, three poems and five book reviews.[93]

Scott grappled with his uncertain future. Most of his friends had graduated and were already forging careers; others had volunteered to fight in the war even though the United States had yet to enter the conflict in Europe. He had ideas of going to war. Until then, preoccupied with campus glory, the war had failed to stir him beyond 'a sporting interest in the German dash for Paris'.[94] In search of direction, he visited Bunny Wilson in New York who was living in an elegant Washington Square apartment. He saw the city in a new light, beyond the style and glitter of casual visits.[95]

He took the counsel of Father Fay and Shane Leslie, whom he met frequently over the following months. His notes of the time mention, 'Fay's silk pajamas'. On one occasion, he discussed Somerset Maugham's *Our Betters* with Mrs Leslie, a satirical comedy about the interaction of nouveau riche Americans with upper-class British society. Leslie had been invalided out of the British Ambulance Corps and returned to America on a diplomatic mission to neutralise nationalist Irish opposition to the United States entering the war on the side of England. He also sought President Woodrow Wilson's support to pressure British Prime Minister Lloyd George into implementing Home Rule in Ireland.

When America finally entered the war in April 1917, Scott evocatively captured its encroachment.

> Slowly and inevitably, yet with a sudden surge at the last, war rolled swiftly up the beach and washed the sands where Princeton played. Every night the gymnasium echoed as platoon after platoon swept over the floor and shuffled out the basket-ball markings.[96]

His life decision dilemma was temporarily postponed and his weak academic record mended when he agreed to undergo three weeks intensive military training as part of a programme offering college students full credit for dropped courses. He wrote to Ceci Taylor in June, 'Had I met Shane Leslie when I last saw you? Well, I've seen a lot more of him – He's an author and a perfect knockout.' Scott encouraged her to read two of his books, *The End of a Chapter* and *The Celt and the World*, adding 'you'd enjoy them both immensely'.[97]

Scott found *The End of a Chapter* to be 'very entertaining'. Written while he was recuperating in hospital, Leslie addressed the key geopolitical, cultural and religious trends emerging in advance of the war and the state of the British Empire and Ireland. Dedicating the book to Captain Norman Leslie, his brother whom he buried in Armentières, he interpreted the war between England and Germany as the suicide of Christian civilisation and expressed regret that Parnell had been toppled as leader of the Irish Parliamentary Party. He wrote romantically, and somewhat condescendingly, of Ireland being a land of peasant wisdom, stalked by beauty and mystery.

But it was Leslie's *The Celt and the World* that resonated most with Scott. In his study of the historical relationship between the Celt and the Teuton, Leslie placed both on an equal racial footing, describing them as the 'first and second born' of the Aryan race. He framed the mystical Celt as the underdog in the age-old conflict with the materialistic Teuton. So inspired was Scott by the book, he reviewed it in the *Nassau Lit.*

The Celt and the World is a sort of bible of Irish patriotism. Mr. Leslie has endeavored to trace a race, the Bretton, Scotch, Welsh, and Irish Celt, through its spiritual crises and he emphasizes most strongly the trait that Synge, Yeats and Lady Gregory have made so much of in their plays, the Celt's inveterate mysticism.

Scott appreciated the mocking tone towards Teutonic ethical standards:

> The theme is worked out in an era-long contrast between Celt and Teuton, and the book becomes ever ironical when it deals of [*sic*] the ethical values of the latter race. 'Great is the Teuton indeed,' it says, 'Luther in religion, Bessemer in steel, Nietzsche in philosophy, Rockefeller in oil – Cromwell and Bismarck in war.' What a wonderful list of names! Could anyone but an Irishman have linked them in such damning significance?[98]

He immersed himself in the works of the leading figures of the Irish Literary Revival – John Millington Synge, William Butler Yeats and Lady Gregory, who provided the cultural bulwark against the materialism of the Anglo-Saxon. Disturbances had accompanied the staging of Synge's *The Playboy of the Western World* in New York in 1911, when Scott was in his first year at Newman. Many Irish-American nationalists, long battling anti-Irish stereotypes, took exception to the portrayal of the Irish people in the play. John Devoy condemned the work as a 'vile libel on Irish womanhood and a gross misrepresentation of their religious feelings' and reportedly stood up during the performance shouting, 'Son of a bitch, that's not Irish.'[99]

The universal themes and timeless tragedy of Leslie's work profoundly impacted Scott. He quoted from the foreword of *The End of a Chapter* that the world was witnessing the end of one era and the beginning of another 'to which no Gods have as yet been rash enough to give their names'. He pointed out that *The Celt and the World* would be 'especially interesting' to those who had enjoyed Synge's *Riders to the Sea* or Yeats' *The Hour-Glass*. Synge's one-act tragedy, set on the Aran Islands off the west coast of Ireland, expressed the hopelessness of the human struggle against the relentless cruelty of the sea and the tension between the traditional and modern. *The Hour-Glass* explored mortality and the fleeting nature of life.

Scott discovered two more Irish authors during this period. In his dramatised account of his time at Princeton, he described his introduction to George Bernard Shaw as 'quite by accident while browsing in the library during mid-years'.[100] The social reform themes of Shaw and of H.G. Wells captivated him. He read Shaw's *Mrs. Warren's Profession*, a play about a brothel madam justifying her career to her daughter.

John Peale Bishop introduced him to Oscar Wilde:

'Ever read any Oscar Wilde?' he asked.

'No. Who wrote it?'

'It's a man – don't you know?'

'Oh, surely.' A faint chord was struck in [his] memory. 'Wasn't the comic opera, "Patience," written about him?'

'Yes, that's the fella. I've just finished a book of his, "The Picture of Dorian Gray," and I certainly wish you'd read it. You'd like it. You can borrow it if you want to.'

Oscar Wilde had been raised with strong Irish nationalist views. His mother, Jane Wilde, wrote poems supporting Irish independence under the pen name, Speranza. His particular appeal to Scott was his criticism of the social expectations and values of the pre-war Victorian upperclass. In *The Picture of Dorian Gray*, the protagonist lives a double life of outward charm and inner corruption, something Scott felt about himself. He was also attracted to Wilde's role in the aesthetic movement that held that art should be produced for the sake of beauty alone, challenging Victorian materialism and the accepted norm that literature and art must have an ethical purpose.

Obsessed with Wilde, and Keats and Swinburne, Scott spent a month strutting around campus trying to look at Princeton through the author's eyes, striving to make every remark an epigram and calling Wilde by his very Irish middle names, Fingal O'Flaherty.[101] His dorm mates were amused. One of them read *Dorian Gray*, simulated Lord Henry Wotton, the man who led Dorian astray, and followed Scott about, addressing him as 'Dorian' and pretending to encourage in him 'wicked fancies and attenuated tendencies to ennui'. When he carried it into Commons, to the amazement of those eating, Scott 'became furiously embarrassed'.

Princeton Patriot

Taking a bold, near revolutionary, stance on the sensitive Irish political question, Scott wrote in his review of *The Celt and the World*: 'At the end of the book that no less passionate and mystical, although unfortunate, incident of Pearse, Plunkett and the Irish Republic, is given sympathetic but just treatment.'

A year earlier during Easter 1916 members of the Irish Volunteers and the Irish Citizen Army seized important buildings in Dublin and proclaimed the birth of the Irish Republic. For six days, the small rebel force held out under persistent bombardment and repeated military assaults until the inevitable surrender order was issued. Patrick Pearse, commander of the rebel forces, and Joseph Mary Plunkett, one of the seven signatories to the Proclamation of the Irish Republic, were not mentioned by Leslie in *The Celt and the World*. Their names were already familiar to Scott.

Leslie opposed the Easter Rising dismissing it as a 'suicidal outburst of a noble idealism' by those who believed they had been deceived by British false promises on granting Home Rule. He called the rebellion a misunderstanding, and in a patronising view of the rebels, attributed it to typical Anglo-Saxon treatment of the Celtic temperament, writing, 'It is impossible for double-dealing to be practised upon so primitive and passionate a mind as the Irish.'

Patrick Pearse held a degree in Arts and Law from the Royal University and was an educationalist, barrister and poet. He travelled to America in 1914 on a fundraising tour for St Enda's, the bilingual boys' school he founded in 1908. Pearse was sentenced to death and executed by firing squad following the 1916 Rising. Joseph Mary Plunkett, son of a papal count, was a poet, journalist and an editor of the influential *Irish Review*. He married artist and cartoonist Grace Gifford in the chapel of Kilmainham jail seven hours before meeting his firing squad. Sixteen Irish leaders were executed. Plunkett's aide-de-camp, Michael Collins, emerged as one of a new generation that took their place.

Scott's mild condemnation of the Easter Rising as an unfortunate incident and praise for the military action as passionate and mystical was not a consensus view. Anglo-Americans criticised the action of the Irish rebels as pro-German and his review appeared amid rising anti-German hysteria when America entered the war.

Many Americans believed their country had no right to interfere in the Irish question, which they considered a domestic matter for England. Many equated Irish independence with the secession of the Confederacy. Some sympathised with the loyal and industrious Ulster protestants falling under the yoke of a Catholic majority, even fearing religious persecution. Others believed an independent Ireland would lead to 'an orgy of legislation, in jobbery, and in financial ruin … an Irish Tammany Hall'.[102]

Though the rebellion was widely criticised, the executions of the leaders sparked outrage across the political spectrum in America. Senator William Borah, a Republican from Idaho, deplored the 'midnight judgements' of the courts martial sitting in Dublin. Father Fay was among the many voices urging the British government to commute the death sentences.

The executions led to a remarkable shift in political views on Ireland. Home Rule supporters in America, the dominant political opinion before the war, had coalesced around the middle-class United Irish League. After decades of campaigning, the Westminster parliament had finally passed legislation in 1914 granting Home Rule to Ireland, but its implementation was suspended until after the war.

The suspension exasperated many Irish-Americans, already disillusioned by repeated English broken promises, mooted proposals for the partitioning of Ireland, and the appointment of Edward Carson – leader of the Ulster Unionists – to the British war cabinet. The execution of the leaders dramatically reshaped opinion. William Bourke Cockran, a member of the House of Representatives, a lawyer and famed orator, spoke of his conversion from Home Rule to the cause of an Irish Republic in the wake of the executions:

For thirty years I have been one of those who had believed
... that it was the part of prudence for Irishmen to forget ...
the wrongs of the centuries in the hope that better days were
dawning ... And now, behold the consequences of this attempt
... The noblest Irishmen that have ever lived are dead, dead
by the bullet of British soldiery, shot like dogs for asserting the
immortal truths of patriotism![103]

The day after Bourke Cockran delivered this impassioned speech, the president of the United Irish League
cabled John Redmond, leader of the Home Rule-sup-
porting Irish Parliamentary Party, that the executions had
'alienated every American friend and caused a resurgence
of ancient enmities. Your life work destroyed by English
brutality.' The once-dominant United Irish League was
a spent force, replaced by the pro-independence Friends
of Irish Freedom, co-founded and led by Daniel F. Cohalan, a justice of the Supreme Court of New York. In a
remarkable transformation, the nebulous goal of an Irish
republic had rapidly shifted from the realm of a small
group of conspiracists to the forefront of mainstream
American politics.

While Bourke Cockran's political views evolved, Fay
and Leslie remained steadfast Home Rulers. During May
1917 both participated in an innovative symposium on an
English proposal for a special convention on Home Rule
in Dublin. Initiated through the letters page of the liberal
Evening Post, the symposium sought the views of leading
Irish-Americans, rather like an online forum today.

Expressing his support for the convention, Father Fay declared, 'I cannot see how any one of Irish blood could refuse … Our whole contention for the past seven hundred years has been that if the English would let us alone we could settle our own difficulties.'[104] On the opposite side of the debate, Judge Cohalan saw the convention as a 'cunningly devised proposal' designed to convince the American public of English sincerity in claiming to fight for the rights of small nations.

Shane Leslie and Bourke Cockran remained close friends notwithstanding their opposing political views. They were married to sisters – daughters of Henry Clay Ide, the American ambassador to Spain and former governor general to the Philippines. Cockran was a mentor to the young Winston Churchill, Leslie's first cousin, and a reputed lover of his American-born mother. When Churchill was en route to cover the war of independence in Cuba, Bourke Cockran invited him to stay at his 300-acre Cedar estate on Long Island. Churchill later paid tribute to his host during his Iron Curtain speech, praising him as 'a great Irish-American orator, a friend of mine'.[105]

Leslie invited Scott to visit Bourke Cockran's opulent home, his first exposure to the great houses clustered on Long Island and the lavish lifestyles of their owners. Like other Irish-American writers, the motif of the Big House became a recurring theme. The budding writer must have left an impression on the famous orator when he demonstrated his verbal agility in a late-night oration to Bourke Cockran's dog, climaxing with the declaration, 'A man only wants to know for certain that his children are his own!'[106]

Once America entered the war on the side of England, President Wilson sought to secure immediate implementation of self-government in Ireland. His motivation was the persuasion of young American men of Irish blood to fight side by side with England as an ally in a war sold to them as a fight for the freedom of small nations. Wilson was concerned about the close ties that had developed between Irish-Americans and their German counterparts. In *The Celt and the World*, Leslie advocated for breaking this 'Irish-German entente'. For years before the war, Irish and German immigrant communities had united to resist the increasing anglicisation of American society. Wilson urged British Prime Minister Lloyd George to grant Ireland a substantial measure of self-government, stating, 'Successful action now would absolutely divorce our citizens of Irish birth and sympathy from the German sympathizers here.'[107] The British took no action.

Meanwhile, many Irish men enlisted in the British Army believing their service and sacrifice would lead to certain implementation of the Home Rule Act after the war as promised. One of those, Major William Redmond, a friend of Shane Leslie, was killed at the Battle of Messines Ridge on 7 June. Redmond (56) was an Irish MP and leading member of the Irish Parliamentary Party. As a young man he had joined the Land League alongside Parnell, sharing a cell with him in Kilmainham Gaol for three months and touring America raising funds in 1882.

Leslie reflected on the death of his friend in the field as 'one of the most dramatic and pathetic events in the war'. He neatly summed up Redmond's political life fighting for Home Rule: 'For a quarter of a century he had represented the stony hills of Clare in the stonier wastes of Westminster.'[108] When Leslie ran for parliament in 1910 as a candidate for the Irish Parliamentary Party, John Redmond, the leader, and William's elder brother, launched his campaign. Leslie narrowly lost in two elections that year to a Unionist opponent of Home Rule, the first time by just fifty-seven votes. As in America, support for Home Rule in Ireland was on the wane. In a subsequent by-election for William Redmond's parliament seat, Éamon de Valera, one of the 1916 leaders who had not been executed, won a landslide victory.

Scott noted in his ledger for June: 'Deal Beach. Russia? Swim. Willie Remond [*sic*].' On a visit to Father Fay's family home at Deal Beach, the priest asked Scott to join him on a mission to Russia to restore the country to Catholic unity.[109] Russia had experienced the first of its two revolutions in February resulting in the abdication of the Tsar. Scott considered the proposal over the following months. His inclusion of Willie Redmond in the ledger, with a typographical error, indicates the impact the death of the Irish patriot had on him.

Three days later, in his letter to Ceci Taylor, written as he prepared to go to his second army training camp, he included four poems for her review and exclaimed 'Damn this war!' in frustration at the disruption to his literary pursuits. With the war weighing heavily on his mind, he revealed his foreboding for the future of his generation.

> On the whole I'm having a fairly good time – but it looks as if the youth of me and my generation ends sometime during the present year, rather summarily – If we ever get back, and I don't particularly care, we'll be rather aged – in the worst way. After all, life hasn't much to offer except youth …[110]

He did not doubt the war aims, but he explained to Ceci that he had no time for blind patriotism, and in doing so, declared himself an Irishman.

> Every man I've met who's been to war – that is this war – seems to have lost youth and faith in man unless they're wine-bibbers of patriotism which, of course, I think is the biggest rot in the world. Updike of Oxford or Harvard says 'I die for England' or 'I die for America' – not me.
> I'm too Irish for that – I may get killed for America – but I'm going to die for myself.

He developed the patriotic theme in a story, 'Sentiment – and the Use of Rouge', written for the June issue of the *Nassau Lit*. In the climactic scene, an Irish sergeant lies gravely wounded in a crater in No Mans Land.

Beside him is an aristocratic English officer, also mortally wounded. The sergeant contrasts the attitude of the English and the Irish to death.

> You see when an English bye dies he does some play actin'
> before. Blood on an Englishman always calls rouge to me
> mind. It's a game with him. The Irish take death damn seri-
> ous.
> … I may get killed for me flag, but I'm goin' to die for meself.

In concluding his review of *The Celt and the World*, Scott issued a proclamation of his own Irish identity: 'To an Irishman, the whole book is fascinating. It gives one an intense desire to see Ireland free at last to work out her own destiny under Home Rule.'

He started to sign letters 'Gaelicly yours' and 'God bless you, Celticly.'[111] When he sent a spare photo to Bunny Wilson, he declared: 'It looks rather Teutonic but I can prove myself a Celt.'[112]

RED SCARE

Awaiting his commission, Scott spent July writing poetry with John Peale Bishop at his family home in Charleston.[113] He sent twelve of his poems to various magazines making a deal with himself, 'If I get them all back I'm going to give up poetry and turn to prose.'[114] A literary magazine accepted one of the poems, but it was not published.

Returning to St Paul at the end of the month, he passed the remainder of the summer drinking gin and reading philosophy, most of the time 'bored to death'.[115] He took army exams at Fort Snelling and in August learned that Jack Newlin, who had left Princeton to volunteer in the American Field Ambulance Service, and had the potential to be a 'great artist', had been killed in France.[116] His friend Bishop was stationed at Fort Benjamin Harrison in Indiana and Wilson was in the war 'at close quarters'.[117]

Scott gave serious consideration to accompanying Father Fay on his Russian mission. 'The conversion of Russia has already begun,' the priest wrote excitedly. 'Several millions of Russians have already come over to the Catholic Church.'[118] Claiming support from the State Department and the British Foreign Office, Fay updated Scott on his plan. They would enter the country under the cover of a Red Cross commission. Fay would arrange for him to share his cabin on the ship and a room when they arrived in Russia, 'as it will save some money at least and give us a chance to talk the things over which must be strictly confidential between us'. Revelling in the role of international man of mystery, he added, 'As soon as you have read this letter and shown it at home, burn it. With best love.' Scott applied for a passport, despite Russia experiencing widespread unrest and food shortages. Fortunately, Fay cancelled the mission at the last moment. Shortly after, the Bolsheviks took control in the October Revolution, initiating the first 'Red Scare' in America.

On another visit to the Fay family home at Deal Beach, the priest invited him to Rome as his private secretary on a diplomatic mission as Cardinal Gibbons' representative to the Vatican. Outlining the plan in a letter to Bunny Wilson, Scott expressed his pride in the large number of Irish Catholics serving under General Pershing in the American Expeditionary Forces: 'I can go to Italy If I like as private secretary of a man (a priest) who is going as Cardinal Gibbons [*sic*] representative to discuss the war with the Pope (American Catholic point of view – which is most loyal – barring the Sien-Fien [*sic*] – 40% of Pershing's army are Irish Catholics).'[119] He unfairly categorised nationalist Irish-Americans as disloyal; the majority had wrapped themselves in the flag once America entered the conflict.

Still waiting his commission in September, he returned to Princeton to complete his senior year, rooming in Campbell Hall with John Biggs, the son of the Attorney

General of Delaware and a future circuit judge. Biggs was the editor of the *Tiger* and Scott wrote pieces for the humour magazine and the *Nassau Lit.*[120] As autumn advanced and he continued to be 'rather bored', he enjoyed meeting Shane Leslie occasionally.[121]

With time on his hands, Scott shared a timeline of his favourite authors' ages with Wilson, 'Do you realize that Shaw is 61, Wells 51, Chesterton 41, Leslie 31 and I 21?' Though made in jest, he took pleasure in placing himself in such exalted literary company. He added: 'Too bad I haven't a better man for 31. I can hear your addition to this remark.' Even Leslie would have admitted to not being in the same literary league as Shaw, Wells and G.K. Chesterton. When Scott sent the same timeline to him, he described it as 'all the great authors of the world in arithmetical progression'.[122]

Scott shared his opinion with Wilson on the divisive New York mayoral election campaign: 'If Hillquit gets the mayoralty of New York it means a new era.'[123] Morris Hillquit, a labour lawyer and founding member of the Socialist Party of America, was running on an anti-war platform. That Scott believed a socialist could become mayor of New York reflected rising radicalism in American urban politics. An election battle for the soul of the city and a referendum on the war, the mayoral campaign pitted the underdog Hillquit against John Purroy Mitchel, the incumbent mayor, reform advocate and war supporter, and John F. Hylan, a Tammany Hall Democrat.

Irish nationalists, including Judge Cohalan, backed the candidacy of Hylan, a former railroad worker turned lawyer, over the aloof and Ivy League-educated Mitchel, a Home Rule supporter despite an impressive Irish republican lineage through his grandfather. During a mass meeting at Madison Square Garden in support of Mitchel, Theodore Roosevelt made a public attack on the loyalty of Cohalan, denouncing the 'Huns within' as being more dangerous than the 'Huns without'. Weeks earlier, just three months after American combat troops had landed in France and during the Third Battle of Ypres (Passchendaele), the *New York Times* had branded Cohalan a traitor to America in a front-page headline screaming, 'Cohalan And Other Irish Leaders Named In New Expose Of German Plots'.

During a raid on the office of German spy Wolf von Igel, the secret service seized incriminating papers. The Committee of Public Information, George Creel's formidable government propaganda agency, released the documents to the press. The *New York Times* published an image of a translated communication from Cohalan to Berlin that had been dictated to von Bernstorff, German Ambassador to America. The document called on German support for the Easter Rising including aerial attacks on England, a diversion of the fleet, and the landing of troops, arms and ammunition in Ireland from Zeppelins. 'This would enable the Irish ports to be closed against England and the establishment of stations for submarines on the Irish coast,' urged Cohalan in the communication, 'and the cutting off of food from England.'

The release of the document was part of a deliberate strategy to discredit Cohalan and others who had opposed America's entry into the war and to negatively impact Hylan's mayoral campaign. The communication was dated 17 April 1916, seven days before the Easter Rising and one year before the United States Congress agreed to join the conflict. While Cohalan was not guilty of treason, he was potentially in breach of the Neutrality Act; according to this, any instruction sent within the United States to begin, set in motion or prepare a military or naval expedition or enterprise was subject to a fine of $3,000, or imprisonment for up to three years.

In response, Cohalan issued a statement condemning the report as a British plot similar to the attempt to discredit Parnell with forged letters and Roger Casement with a forged diary. He cited a warning given to him in May 1916 'by one who had entry to the British Embassy' that the British authorities were determined if possible to 'destroy' him, and another warning given a year later at a meeting in the embassy attended by Shane Leslie.

The attack by former President Roosevelt was a step too far for Cohalan. Declaring that he was an American 'who yields to no man in devotion to this country', he came out fighting in a statement published in the *New York Times*:

The man, I care not who he may be, who says that I have
ever had a disloyal thought … is false and the truth is not in
him. I am thoroughly American … I am with her in this war
against Germany … I made it clear and unmistakable from
the platform of Carnegie Hall within forty-eight hours after
the declaration of war.[124]

The *New York Times* continued its attack in an incrim-
inatory editorial, 'The Cohalan Evidence'.[125] The press
campaign continued through the winter until a libel suit
against the publisher of the *Evening Mail* was settled in
his favour. Media criticism ended and impeachment
proceedings in the New York Senate came to nothing.[126]
However, the document released by George Creel was
indeed authentic. Cohalan had requested that a telegram
be sent to Berlin on his behalf by von Bernstorff and a
copy was retained in the German diplomatic archives in
Berlin.[127] Shane Leslie accurately assessed Cohalan as
'ready to go to any length and to make any alliance in
furtherance of an Irish Republic'.[128]

During the mayoral campaign, the left-leaning Irish
Progressive League was formed to support Hillquit. The
New York group had a core membership of 150 labour,
socialist, suffragist and liberal activists, many of whom
were born in Ireland. Unlike Cohalan and the Friends of
Irish Freedom during the war, they were openly critical of
Britain, America's wartime ally, and Wilson, the wartime
president.[129] The Friends of Irish Freedom had pledged
loyalty to America once she entered the war. The organi-

sation toned down criticism of Britain and dropped overt German–American connections, focusing instead on building an organisation powerful enough to have influence in post-war Washington.

In the final two weeks of the election campaign, Hillquit gained unexpected momentum. As well as socialist support, he attracted pro-war liberals protesting against government curbs on press freedom.[130] The Democratic Party shifted its heavy political artillery from an assault on Mitchel to an attack on the Socialist candidate. On election day, Hylan secured a comfortable victory, though Hillquit won 22 per cent of the citywide vote. Scott's new socialist era did not materialise.

The Beginning and End of Everything

Finally receiving his commission as a second lieutenant in October 1917, Scott was assigned to the infantry officers' training camp at Fort Leavenworth, Kansas. The twenty-one-year-old advised his concerned mother that, 'If you want to pray, pray for my soul and not that I won't get killed – the last doesn't seem to matter particularly and if you are a good Catholic the first ought to.'[131]

Fearing he would have only three months to live once in the field, he was determined to leave his mark on the world by writing an 'immortal novel'.[132] Not permitting a 'mere war' to derail his plan, he spent each evening at Fort Leavenworth discreetly writing in a pad concealed behind his infantry instruction manual. When detected by superiors, leaving only weekends to complete the novel, every Saturday afternoon when the week's work was over he hurried to the Officers' Club to write at breakneck speed in a corner of a roomful of smoke, conversation and rattling newspapers.[133]

Though aspiring to be a miliary hero, he was not cut out to be a leader of men; he was self-absorbed, distracted and lacking the personal skills to engage meaningfully with his troops. A poor officer, he managed to avoid the wrath of his captain, Dwight D. Eisenhower.[134] 'The prevailing attitude toward Fitzgerald,' a fellow officer recalled, 'was that if we were given an important task and told he would be assigned to help us, we would prefer to do it alone. This attitude implied no hostility toward Fitzgerald. Indeed most of us liked him.'[135]

Early in the New Year Scott proudly wrote to Wilson, already his intellectual conscience, that his novel 'rather damns much of Princeton but it's nothing to what it thinks of men and human nature in general'.[136] He informed his friend with confidence that if *The Romantic Egoist*, his preferred title for the book, was published, 'I'll wake some morning and find that the debutantes have made me famous over-night. I really believe that no one else could have written so searchingly the story of the youth of our generation.'

He worked full time on the novel on a week's leave at Princeton. Shane Leslie corrected punctuation and grammar before sending it to his own publisher, Charles Scribner's Sons. In his cover letter, Leslie introduced the writer as 'a friend of mine and a descendant of the author of the Star spangled banner'. Although seeing scope to reduce the novel by a third, Leslie was impressed with Scott's young voice: '… it has given me a vivid picture of the American generation that is hastening to war. I marvel at its crudity and its cleverness. It is naive in places, shocking in others, painful to the conventional … I knew the poetic Rupert Brooke and this is a prose one

… It interests me as a boy's book and I think gives expression to … real American youth …'[137]

In May, expecting to be shipped to France within two months, Scott thanked Leslie for 'writing that awfully decent letter to Scribner'.[138] In June he reported to Camp Sheridan in Alabama for final preparations before embarkation. Officers swarmed the nearby town of Montgomery seeking one last chance at romance. At a dance at the Country Club of Montgomery, handsome in his officer's uniform, Scott cut a dashing figure. An admirer of the confederacy, he might have pictured himself as a civil war officer preparing for battle sixty years earlier, within living memory of some in the town. One local girl with a talent for florid writing observed Scott arriving at the country club: 'There seemed to be some heavenly support beneath his shoulder blades that lifted his feet from the ground in ecstatic suspension, as if he secretly enjoyed the ability to fly but was walking as a compromise to convention.'[139]

Scott noticed the girl and sought an introduction. She was Zelda Sayre, the daughter of an episcopalian justice of the Alabama Supreme Court and a recent high school graduate voted 'prettiest and most attractive' by her class.[140] Throw in her distinguished confederate lineage, including a great-uncle who had been a Southern general and later United States senator, and it is easy to understand status-hungry Scott's interest. Free spirited and self-assured, with a wild, pleasure-loving and reckless streak, Zelda was no ordinary girl. She drank, smoked and was a notorious flirt. The officers were infatuated with her. Most had never met a girl like Zelda. Aviators daringly buzzed the family home of Montgomery's most popular girl to get her attention.[141] But she was more impressed with Scott's heavenly levitation on the dance floor, though nothing was ever guaranteed when it came to winning her hand.

Infatuated and falling in love, Scott took the bus into Montgomery at every opportunity. He telephoned every day and twice daily when he was unable to leave the base. Though both had an exhibitionistic streak, there was a difference, as one biographer noted: 'Fitzgerald wanted admiration or at least attention; Zelda did not care what people thought. His behavior indicated insecurity; hers seemed to display indifference or defiance.'[142]

To ascend to her hand, Scott had to pass a stern gate-keeper in the austere Judge Anthony Dickinson Sayre, sixty years old and a 'living fortress' in Zelda's eyes. Mrs Sayre, more liberal than her husband and genuinely fond of Scott, nevertheless cautioned her daughter on the perils of marrying an impoverished writer.[143] Zelda might have been charmed by her striking lieutenant, but the Sayres saw through the invisible cloak of his military uniform to the empty bank account and his unstable future career as a writer. Their daughter required a reliable husband to temper her wild impulses.

Then there was the not-inconsiderable problem that Scott was Irish and Catholic. Zelda's biographer described the social environment he attempted to enter:

'For in Montgomery it was never simply wealth that counted socially, but family. There were very definite lines of social distinction; one was not invited to parties on The Hill if one was in trade, or Catholic, or Italian, or Shanty Irish.'[144] Scott's drinking also made a poor impression on Judge Sayre, a strict teetotaller. Zelda once said to her father that Scott was the sweetest person in the world when sober, to which the judge replied, 'He's never sober.'[145]

Winning over Judge Sayre might have appeared another quixotic challenge after his experience with the aristocratic Charles Garfield King. However, the moderately wealthy Sayres of Montgomery posed a less daunting challenge. His courteous manners and sense of honour, values instilled by his father, counted in southern society. As for family and religion, the Ashton Keys, albeit Catholic, had a southern lineage at least as prestigious as the Sayres. Likewise, he could present the McQuillans as upper middle-class Irish. And he was now a lieutenant in the United States Army about to ship overseas. He must have kept hidden his newly discovered pride in his Celtic heritage and interest in Ireland; in the South there was little sympathy for the Irish cause.

At the same time as meeting Zelda, Scott reconnected with Ginevra King for the first time since their breakup eighteen months earlier. Perhaps he hoped for one last chance before going off to war. Glad to learn that he had not been killed in France, Ginevra shared the 'wonderful news' of her engagement to William 'Billie' Mitchell.[146]

Wanting a quick marriage, she was eager to join her fiancé, now a naval aviator ensign stationed in Key West. The latter detail rubbed salt in Scott's wounded heart, as he too had wanted to serve as an aviator. Ironically, at that moment, the editors at Scribner were reading of his ambition:

'Infantry or aviation, I can't make up my mind – I hate mechanics, but then of course aviation's the thing for me –'

'… aviation sounds like the romantic side of the war, of course – like cavalry used to be ...'[147]

Ginevra King, daughter of the president of the stock-broking firm King, Farnum & Co., married William Mitchell, son of the president of the Illinois Trust & Savings Bank, on 4 September. Heartbroken, Scott pasted Ginevra's photograph and a newspaper clipping of her marriage into his scrapbook. At the bottom of the page, he wrote, 'The End of a Once Poignant Story.' This was a futile attempt at closure because he could not shake the feeling that the wealthy upper class had exercised 'a sort of droit de seigneur' over his girl.[148] On the rebound, three days after the wedding, as he later noted, he 'Fell in love' with Zelda.[149]

He received another blow when Scribner rejected *The Romantic Egoist*. However, Maxwell Perkins, a new progressive member of the editorial staff, wrote to him that they had read the novel with 'a very unusual degree of interest' and that they had not seen a novel 'display so much originality' in a long time.[150] Perkins had been tasked with developing contemporary talent at the traditionally conservative publishing house. Scott's candid coming of age novel, filled with rebellious baby vamps, petting parties, jazz music and girls full of the devil was not to everyone's taste. One member of the sales department frequently deferred opinion on new books to an erudite sister.

His sister was supposed to be infallible and it was true that many of the novels she had 'cried over' sold prodigiously. So when it was known that he had taken … [the book] … home for the week-end, his colleagues were agog on Monday morning. 'And what did your sister say?' they asked in chorus. 'She picked it up with the tongs,' he replied, 'because she wouldn't touch it with her hands after reading it, and put it into the fire.'[151]

The Romantic Egoist was unstructured with mixed narrators and styles; the script had poetry interludes, stage play scenes and was filled with cultural, philosophical, political and social references, many of them obscure. Scott admitted to Leslie that the 'novel has been scattered into shape – for it has no form to speak of'.[152] However, recognising that much of the prose was magnificent and the voice unique, Perkins offered constructive and encouraging advice, and invited him to revise and resubmit the novel.[153] He reworked the manuscript over the following weeks, but to no avail. In October, Perkins sent a telegram with the disappointing news that the book had been rejected again. Scott added the telegram to his scrapbook with a note: 'The end of a dream.'[154]

In late October, on receiving his overseas orders, Scott was sent to Camp Mills on Long Island. Awaiting embarkation to France, he partied wildly in New York City, riding a horse cab through Times Square to the thrill of his friends, cartwheeling through a bar, and being caught naked in a hotel bedroom with a girl by the house detective.[155] Scott's dream of battlefield glory ended with the signing of the armistice with Germany on 11 November.

Shipped back to Camp Sheridan, he was appointed aide-de-camp to Brigadier General James Augustine Ryan who was in charge of relations with the civil authorities. For once, his Irish Catholic heritage had worked in his favour. Unexpectedly back in Montgomery, he had decisions to make about his future, especially concerning Zelda. 'My affair still drifts,' he confided to Ruth Sturtevant. 'But my mind is firmly made up that I will not, shall not, cannot, should not, must not marry, – still, she is remarkable – I'm trying desperately exire armis [to exit valorously].'[156]

His doubts did not survive their first Christmas together. During his favourite time of the year, they fell madly in love; sharing long walks in the woods and dancing away the evenings together. Though concerned about her wild behaviour, he had fallen in love with her 'courage, her sincerity and her flaming self-respect', traits that he believed lacking in himself. 'I love her and that's the beginning and end of everything.'[157]

BREAKING POINT

A third wave of the deadly influenza pandemic, commonly known as the Spanish flu, swept through the country over the winter. Father Fay succumbed to pneumonia complications in January 1919. Desolate at the loss of a father figure, Scott poured out his grief to Leslie, 'He was the best friend I had in the world.'[158] Leslie, so ill that he had to practically crawl to the funeral, replied that Scott should take holy orders and offered himself as a replacement surrogate father, declaring, 'Mgr Fay intended leaving you to me in his will. "Son, behold thy father – Father, receive thy son –"?'[159] Scott contracted the virus and replied from the Camp Sheridan base hospital that he was 'nearly sure' of becoming a priest.[160] But he was only placating his literary mentor. All Scott's inherited and learned belief systems and philosophies bowed before a new deity, as he later wrote: 'Zelda's the only God I have left now.'

On his demobilisation in February, he dangled the dream of a new life in New York before her; he would get a job and write stories at night to establish his reputation. Notwithstanding the exciting prospect of leaving small-town Montgomery for the glamour of a city she had never visited, Zelda hesitated in committing her future to an insolvent writer whose first novel had been twice rejected. Her mother's advice had not gone unheeded.

Arriving in New York full of confidence and enthusiasm, he immediately wired her: 'I am in the land of ambition and success, and my only hope and faith, is that my darling heart will be with me soon.'[161] With victory in the air and on the cusp of the Jazz Age, New York as he later wrote 'had all the iridescence of the beginning of the world ... returning troops marched up Fifth Avenue and girls were instinctively drawn east and north towards them – we were at last admittedly the most powerful nation and there was gala in the air.'[162] His desire to emulate Bunny Wilson by taking an apartment in Greenwich Village, however, met the reality of his precarious financial position. While waiting for Zelda to make a decision, he settled for a place on the Upper West Side, 'one room in a high, horrible apartment-house in the middle of nowhere'.[163]

After failing to convince seven city editors of the seven newspapers in New York to give him a job as a reporter, he had to settle for a position as a copywriter for the Barron Collier advertising agency. By day, he turned out banal commercial slogans, and by night he wrote short stories to sell to magazines. Towards the end of March, fearing that Zelda's ardour was waning, he sent his mother's engagement ring to Montgomery. He wrote a formal letter to Judge Sayre requesting his daughter's hand in marriage, but she was too nervous to give the letter to her father. Her mother, meanwhile, continued to badger her with 'subtle suggestions' about the precarious life of aspiring writers.[164]

Though not formally engaged, they accepted the engagement as a fact. 'I am so proud to be your girl – to have everybody know we are in love.' Zelda wrote after creating 'havoc' when she wore the ring to a dance. 'It's so good to know you're always loving me … and I want to be married soon – soon.' Her vibrant social life with male friends gave him anxiety. 'Lover – Don't say I'm not enthusiastic,' she reassured him with a hint of reproach. 'You ought to know.'[165] As spring turned to summer, his dream of achieving success in New York stalled. He loathed his job, earned barely enough to support himself and had sunk to writing slogans for a laundry in Muscatine, Iowa: 'We Keep You Clean in Muscatine.'[166] He was tired of writing 'painful half-hearted imitations of popular literature' in the evenings. Nineteen short stories written between April and June remained unpublished. In mocking despair, he pinned 122 rejection slips in a frieze around his cheerless room.[167]

While Scott was failing, New York was humming. Returning Ivy League friends, most of whom had served overseas, swapped stories and life plans during exciting post-war reunions. They drank together at the Plaza Red Room, attended lush and liquid garden parties, tippled at the Biltmore Bar and received invitations for atmospheric events at the homes of millionaires. But he hovered 'ghost-like' at these gatherings, there but not there.

I was haunted always by my other life – my drab room … my square foot of the subway, my fixation upon the day's letter from Alabama – would it come and what would it say? – my shabby suits, my poverty, and love … I bought cheap theatre seats at Gray's drugstore and tried to lose myself for a few hours in my old passion for Broadway. I was a failure – mediocre at advertising work and unable to get started as a writer.[168]

Letters to Zelda were his only pleasure and her replies a lifeline. When she struggled to match the intensity of his daily correspondence, he turned to drink in a haze of anxiety and self-absorbed paranoia.[169] As it became less and less likely that the engagement would lead to marriage, he made the journey to Montgomery on three successive months to reassure her. During his final trip in June, she broke off the engagement despite his begging, pleading and a humiliating monologue of self-pity. Leaving Zelda at the train station, he climbed into a sleeper carriage, and sneaked through into the day coach, which was all he could afford for the return trip.[170] He described the relationship as 'one of those tragic loves doomed for lack of money, and one day the girl closed it out on the basis of common sense'.

Left with an 'abiding distrust, an animosity toward the leisure class – not the conviction of a revolutionist but the smoldering hatred of a peasant,' he arrived back in New York a different person.[171] Holed up in his one room apartment during a stifling heat wave, he reached breaking point. 'I've done my best and I've failed,' he laid bare to Ruth Sturtevant. 'It's a great tragedy to me and I feel I have very little left to live for … Unless someday she will marry me I will never marry.'[172] Being poor in New York was unbearable. 'It's a bad town unless you're on top of it.'[173] As the temperature soared and his prospects dived, he went on an epic three-week bender to shield himself from stabs of memory.

> He awoke laughing and his eyes lazily roamed his surround-ings, evidently a bedroom and bath in a good hotel. His head was whirring and picture after picture was forming and blur-ring and melting before his eyes, but beyond the desire to laugh he had no entirely conscious reaction. He reached for the 'phone beside his bed. 'Hello – what hotel is this –? Knick-erbocker? All right, send up two rye high-balls –'[174]

On 1 July, he woke up physically exhausted, but he was over the first flush of pain. 'Since I last saw you I've tried to get married,' he wrote to Wilson, 'and then tried to drink myself to death'.[175] Three days later, on Indepen-dence Day, he abandoned his grey apartment, quit his copywriting job and fled New York in despair. Returning to St Paul a failure, he moved back in with his parents.

COCA-COLA AND
CIGARETTES

Cramped into his sweltering bedroom on the top floor of the rented home in a three-storey brownstone row house on Summit Avenue, while abstaining from alcohol, Scott launched into another re-write of his twice-rejected novel. With so much dependent on its success, desperately and feverishly, and fueled by Coca-Cola and cigarettes supplied by his friend Tubby Washington – because his parents would not fund him as he refused to get a proper job – he embarked on an all or nothing mission to prove he could become a successful and admired writer, and in the process win Zelda back.[176] The heartbreak of losing her was 'still bleeding as fresh as the skin wound on a haemophile'.[177]

Fully immersed in his task and working to a schedule pinned to the curtain in front of his desk, Scott completed the first draft of the novel, retitled *The Education of a Personage*, in just three weeks. On 26 July he wrote to a surprised Max Perkins, explaining, 'It is in no sense a revision of the ill-fated Romantic Egotist, but it contains some of the former material improved and worked over and bears a strong family resemblance besides.'[178] He also incorporated material from earlier short stories. Perkins replied that his unexpected correspondence 'arouses a great curiosity to see the manuscript'.[179]

With a final monumental effort, he completed the novel five weeks later, under another new title, *This Side of Paradise*, inspired by a Rupert Brook poem, 'Well this side of Paradise! ...There's little comfort in the wise.' Scott took the manuscript, wrapped it up, hugged it close, and cried to his friend: 'Tubby! Maybe this is it!'[180]

While anxiously waiting to hear from Perkins, he took a job to make money, as recounted by a St Paul friend who had worked up to a supervisory position in the Northern Pacific carbarn.

> He told Fitzgerald to report in old clothes. Fitzgerald arrived in dirty white flannels, polo shirt, sweatshirt, and a blue cap, and complained ... that he did not seem to be able to make conversation with the men. Eventually he caught on and bought a pair of overalls and learned not to offend the foreman by sitting down when he hammered nails. After a few days, however, he decided he was not cut out for this kind of work and quit.[181]

A letter arrived by special delivery dated 16 September. 'Dear Mr. Fitzgerald, I am very glad, personally, to be able to write to you that we are all for publishing your book.'[182] Scott ran up and down Summit Avenue stopping cars and announcing to whoever would listen that his novel had been accepted for publication, not realising how fortunate he had been to have Perkins in his corner. The innovative editor had to make an impassioned plea for publication in the face of much opposition, arguing, 'If we're going to turn down the likes of Fitzgerald, I will lose all interest in publishing books.' Perkins managed to get *This Side of Paradise* over the line with the help of Charles Scribner, Jr., who persuaded the elder Mr Scribner to accept it. Scott had found a true friend and champion in Perkins: 'I was afraid that, when we declined the first manuscript, you might be done with us conservatives. I am glad you are not … The book is so different that it is hard to prophesy how it will sell but we are all for taking a chance and supporting it with vigor.'

'I KNOW MYSELF, BUT THAT IS ALL'

Max Perkins did not regret taking a chance on Scott. Published in March 1920, *This Side of Paradise* was an instant and surprise success; a literary timebomb that woke America to the existence of a post-war generation refusing to be held back by outdated Victorian expectations, hypocrisy and values: 'Here was a new generation … dedicated more than the last to the fear of poverty and the worship of success; grown up to find all Gods dead, all wars fought, all faiths in man shaken …'

This Side of Paradise was Scott's own story told through a largely autobiographical protagonist, Amory Blaine. A sensation across Ivy League and other colleges, students eagerly sought out the novel that chronicled their unvarnished lives for the first time. The book went through multiple print runs. Scott revealed the source of its success, noting, 'An author ought to write for the youth of his own generation, the critics of the next, and the schoolmasters of ever afterward.'[183]

The novel was of its time, not only in portraying the aspirations and disillusionment of the post-war generation, but in documenting in real time their reaction to unprecedented domestic and global challenges, in particular during the turbulent summer of 1919. Ideological commentary was deliberately naïve and not fully formed, reflecting Scott's own attempt to come to terms with evolving sociopolitical and economic ideologies.

In June 1919, anarchists had detonated large bombs in eight cities across America. On May Day of that year, clashes and riots erupted across major cities, including New York, as communists, socialists, union members, the Industrial Workers of the World and demobbed soldiers took to the streets. Record waves of large-scale industrial strikes, including police, steel and coal workers, broke out. The country was gripped by the Red Scare. Much of the trouble was blamed on emigration from eastern and southern Europe, fuelling anti-foreign sentiment. Shortly after, interracial violence erupted in what newspapers dubbed the Red Summer. The Ku Klux Klan became a political force outside the southern states.

Geopolitically, four empires had collapsed and American eyes turned towards the Pacific to the newly industrialised Japanese Empire. Many predicted war with the Imperial Japanese Army. A week after Scott returned to St Paul to write the novel, a triumphant President Wilson returned from Paris and hand-delivered the Treaty of Versailles, including the controversial League of Nations covenant, to the Senate for ratification, sparking one of the most hostile political debates in American history, which concluded with the United States Senate voting against ratification.

Scott exorcised his bitterness and disillusionment following his romantic rejection by Ginevra and Zelda
through Amory Blaine. His alter ego's first college love,
Isabelle Borge, a sixteen-year-old wealthy debutante, had
a capacity for love affairs that was 'limited only by the
number of the susceptible within telephone distance. His
second love, Rosalind Connage, smokes, drinks and is frequently kissed, and 'treats men terribly'. On the advice of
her mother – 'Now there's a young man I like, and he's
floating in money' – Rosalind rejects Amory and marries
the son of a wealthy family friend. She has redeeming
qualities in her 'fresh enthusiasm, her will to grow and
learn, her endless faith in the inexhaustibility of romance,
her courage and fundamental honesty'.

Much of the social commentary occurs at the end of
the novel, when Amory, broke and fed up in New York, is
offered a lift in a chauffeur-driven car by a successful business man, who is accompanied by his 'artificial growth',
a small anxious man dismissed as a lower secretarial
type. During their discussion, Amory advocates a fair
trial of government ownership of all industries, because
it would mean the 'best analytical business minds in the
government working for something besides themselves'.
He wanted to put James J. Hill 'running interstate com-
merce'. The 'empire builder' receives another favourable
comment in a literary discussion between Amory and
Thomas Parke D'Invilliers, modelled on John Peale
Bishop, when Amory wishes that American novelists
would stop trying to make business romantically interest-

ing: 'Nobody wants to read about it, unless it's crooked business. If it was an entertaining subject they'd buy the life of James J. Hill and not one of these long office trage-dies that harp along on the significance of smoke.'

Amory proposes to the business man the plausibility of making it illegal to have more than a certain amount of money, that men would be happy to be rewarded by honour. 'That's the silliest thing you've said yet,' replies his interlocutor. Amory changes the subject to socialism suggesting that the threat of the red flag is the inspiring force of all reform. He argues, without conviction, that Russia is 'overflowing just as the French Revolution did, but I've no doubt that it's really a great experiment and well worthwhile'. The business man is interested and amused, and Amory reveals the emotional and artistic reasons behind these convictions:

I'm restless. My whole generation is restless. I'm sick of a system where the richest man gets the most beautiful girl if he wants her, where the artist without an income has to sell his talents to a button manufacturer. Even if I had no talents I'd not be content to work ten years, condemned either to celibacy or a furtive indulgence, to give some man's son an automobile.

Earlier in the novel, Amory joked with Princeton friends that they should consider leading contemplative lives, until they had decided to 'use machine-guns with the property owners – or throw bombs with the Bolshevik God!' He admits to selfish reasons for arguing for change: 'My position couldn't be worse. A social revolution might land me on top.' The business man correctly senses that Amory is just a young man trying to find his way:

> 'But you don't believe all this Socialist patter you talk.'
>
> 'I don't know. Until I talked to you I hadn't thought seriously about it. I wasn't sure of half of what I said … I simply state that I'm a product of a versatile mind in a restless generation – with every reason to throw my mind and pen in with the radicals. Even if, deep in my heart, I thought we were all blind atoms in a world as limited as a stroke of a pendulum, I and my sort would struggle against tradition; try, at least, to displace old cants with new ones.'

The road trip ends on a poignant note when the business man learns that Amory and his son, who had been killed in France, were good friends at Princeton.

Like Scott, Amory had reached a point of 'self-reproach and loneliness and disillusion'. In search of identity and his true self, and inspired by the death of Father Fay (Monseigneur Darcy in the novel), he changes his life goals from being admired or loved to being 'necessary to people, to be indispensable … to give people a sense of security'. But, first, he would have to transcend his innate selfishness and lack of 'one drop of the milk of human kindness'. He gives up on religion for the present to 'realize fully the direction and momentum of this new start'.

The novel approaches closure with the elegantly crafted prose that would mark Scott's best writing, full of melancholy for the traditions of old Princeton, while suggesting its unsuitability in serving the aspirations of the new 'chosen youth':

> Long after midnight the towers and spires of Princeton were visible, with here and there a late-burning light – and suddenly out of the clear darkness the sound of bells. As an endless dream it went on; the spirit of the past brooding over a new generation, the chosen youth from the muddled, unchastened world, still fed romantically on the mistakes and half-forgotten dreams of dead statesmen and poets.

Amory has had enough of the value systems espoused by the politicians and poets he used to admire; it had sent a generation to be slaughtered in the fields of France. He'd had enough of God, too. He would make a new start and would find his own way. He still harbours the pain of memory and the regret for his lost youth, but still has 'responsibility and a love of life ... the faint stirring of old ambitions and unrealized dreams'. But thinking out loud – 'oh, Rosalind! Rosalind!' – he considers it all a poor substitute at best. Without knowing why, he is determined to continue the struggle. The last two lines of the novel confirm his new-found, if incomplete, wisdom: 'He stretched out his arms to the crystalline, radiant sky. "I know myself," he cried, "but that is all."'

However, behind the prose mastery, there was little substance. Scott, the writer, was full of contradictions. For all his socialist sympathies, calls for revolution and claims of distrust and animosity toward the leisure class, he – as he revealed later – aspired 'to share their mobility and the grace that some of them brought into their lives'.[184] Whether through fault of nature or nurture, or both, he was a snob.

John Biggs, his room-mate at Princeton, admitted, 'We were all snobs about something … Fitzgerald was a snob's snob. But I think it was to cover up a sense of inferiority.' Another Princeton friend, John D. McMaster, echoed Biggs, 'What Fitzgerald really had in mind, what he felt deep in his own heart was the want of full social acceptance in the nest of the Wasps in which he found himself.'[185] Bunny Wilson observed that the Princeton of their teens 'gave us too much respect for money and country house social prestige … Scott … fell victim to this'.[186]

Other influences also shaped his societal view. Mollie McQuillan passed her unfulfilled social aspirations on to her son, Edward Fitzgerald added his southern pretensions, then Father Fay and Shane Leslie added a layer of flattery and elitism.

Scott had an abiding fear of penury, writing that Amory Blaine was 'afraid of being poor' and experienced the unpleasant aspects of city life without money in 'threatening procession'. Years later, when his daughter was graduating, Scott went to New York to buy fake jewellery, so she could pretend they were graduation presents:

> Otherwise, she will have to suffer the shame of being a poor girl in a rich girl's school. That was always my experience – a poor boy in a rich town; a poor boy in a rich boy's school; a poor boy in a rich man's club at Princeton. So I guess she can stand it. However, I have never been able to forgive the rich for being rich, and it has colored my entire life and works.[187]

He voiced his negative opinion of the struggling working-class in the novel:

> 'I detest poor people,' thought Amory suddenly. 'I hate them for being poor. Poverty may have been beautiful once, but it's rotten now. It's the ugliest thing in the world. It's essentially cleaner to be corrupt and rich than it is to be innocent and poor.'
> He made no self-accusations: never any more did he reproach himself for feelings that were natural and sincere ... This problem of poverty transformed, magnified, attached to some

grander, more dignified attitude might some day even be his problem; at present it roused only his profound distaste.

He seemed to see again a figure whose significance had once impressed him – a well-dressed young man gazing from a club window on Fifth Avenue and saying something to his companion with a look of utter disgust. Probably, thought Amory, what he said was: 'My God! Aren't people horrible!' [Scott is the figure at the window.]

Scott had no empathy for, or understanding of, new arrivals to America. He described a train journey that Amory made shortly after the country went to war:

When Amory went to Washington the next week-end he caught some of the spirit of crisis which changed to repulsion in the Pullman car coming back, for the berths across from him were occupied by stinking aliens – Greeks, he guessed, or Russians. He thought how much easier patriotism had been to a homogeneous race, how much easier it would have been to fight as the Colonies fought, or as the Confederacy fought. And he did no sleeping that night, but listened to the aliens guffaw and snore while they filled the car with the heavy scent of latest America.

Believing in the need for a ruling elite, he wrote that Amory regretted that America had 'no Eton to create the self-consciousness of a governing class'. He questioned why 'the pick of the young Englishmen from Oxford and Cambridge go into politics and in the U.S.A. we leave it to the muckers? – raised in the ward, educated in the assembly and sent to Congress, fat-paunched bundles of corruption, devoid of "both ideas and ideals".' Members of the middle class, represented by the lower secretarial man in the car, were not fit to govern themselves until they could 'be educated to think clearly, concisely, and logically'. The lower classes were 'narrower, less pleasant and personally more selfish – certainly more stupid'. The 'degenerate Italians and illiterate Irish' needed orthodox religion to be 'educated into a moral sense'.

As Scott launched the revolution of the chosen youth of his generation against the Victorian values of their parents, in Ireland, the youth of the country were determined to prove that they could govern themselves, neither wanting nor needing a ruling elite. They looked to Paris, New York and the new emerging nation states in Europe for inspiration. They talked about Irish freedom in a different way, concerned with international trade, taxation, monetary policy, development of internal resources and social improvement. They were determined to break the colonial glass ceiling; the political, economic and social privilege of the governing class, Catholic and Protestant, that would not change under British Rule or Home Rule.

One of their leaders made headlines on his arrival in America when Scott settled down to write *This Side of Paradise* in St Paul during the maelstrom of the summer of 1919.

RETURN OF THE NATIVE

'Oh, he's having a frightful time.'

'Why?' [asked Amory]

'About the Irish Republic. He thinks it lacks dignity.'

F. Scott Fitzgerald, *This Side of Paradise*

While Scott was on his three-week drinking session, roaming between the Biltmore, Maxims and the Knickerbocker bars, a ship steamed into New York. On board was a stowaway; cramped, seasick and with mainly rats for company, Éamon de Valera, President of the self-declared Irish Republic, was spirited off the ship and brought to Rochester to the home of his mother, Mrs Charles Wheelwright. After sending her son to Ireland when he was two years old following the death of his father, his mother had remarried and raised a family. Once settled, de Valera made confidential visits to Joe McGarrity, the publisher of the *Irish Press* in Philadelphia and to the influential Cardinal Gibbons in Baltimore, and he called on several senators in Washington and Irish-American leaders in Boston.

De Valera slipped into America to secure recognition for the new counter-state parliament and government established in Dublin in open defiance of English rule in Ireland. The British government had called an election immediately after the armistice signed with Germany. Sinn Féin, campaigning on Irish independence, won seventy-three out of the 105 seats in Ireland. Instead of going to Westminster, the newly elected representatives set up their own parliament. Over seventy Irish and international journalists were present when the national parliament of the Irish Republic met for the first time on 21 January 1919. A Declaration of Independence was read and a message to the free nations of the world in English and French – 'Aux Nations du Monde! Salut fraternel!'

Michael Collins, Minister for Finance, a twenty-nine-year-old farmer's son and former civil servant, defined the struggle as between 'our determination to govern ourselves and get rid of English rule, and the British determination to prevent us from doing either'.[188] In his dual role as Director of Intelligence, Collins began dismantling the English spy system that kept Ireland under control. Initially, the British government ignored the new assembly, dismissing it variously as a ludicrous farce, a stage play and a piece of political window-dressing. By contrast, George Creel, head of the Committee of Public Information, the American wartime propaganda bureau, compared the assembly to the first session of the Continental Congress: 'Some young and reckless, some old and academic, but for the most part a gathering of very intense patriots with sanely constructive ideas about finance, education, economics, industry, merchant marine, foreign trade.'[189]

The first meeting of the Irish parliament was largely symbolic, lasting just two hours. Many of the Sinn Féin leaders were in prison following their arrest on foot of an alleged 'German Plot'. Accused of 'treasonable communication with the German enemy', they had been interned without trial and deported to England. De Valera escaped in February 1919 and the other leaders were released following the death of a colleague from influenza which was ravaging the English prison system.

The counter-state Irish government had ambitious economic plans, in particular to open direct trading routes between Ireland and America and to re-establish an Irish merchant marine. The native government set up its own Department of Trade, appointed trade consuls overseas and established a 'Commission of Inquiry into the Resources and Industries of Ireland'. Trade opportunities were examined in Europe, Argentina and Chile, and even in Uruguay, Peru and Paraguay.

Two weeks after his arrival in New York, on 23 June, de Valera broke cover to make his first public appearance, addressing fifty reporters gathered in the private reception room of his Waldorf Astoria suite. One reporter noted that de Valera wore glasses and a collar almost of collegian highness, and that he had a scholarly stoop that detracted from his height, a high forehead, deep set brown-black eyes, a rather prominent nose, and a general expression of eagerness.[190] Within days, he changed to a new suite on the eleventh floor that outranked the former apartments 'by many pounds of gilt, a heap more fancy clocks, no end of French vases, and the like'.[191]

Establishing a parallel between the Irish struggle for freedom and the American Revolution, de Valera explained to the reporters that the degree of unanimity in Ireland on independence was 'higher than that claimed by the American colonies when they declared their Independence ... You had your Tories and your Loyalists, too'. He reminded the American public that their revolutionary leaders had been labelled as traitors and murderers, noting, 'so are we'. While they had sought the support of France, de Valera declared, 'We seek the aid of America.' He pointed out that the American nation had come to the aid of the people of Poland, Greece, Hungary and the Latin republics, yet Ireland was 'the one remaining white nation in the slavery of alien rule'. Following a photoshoot on the hotel roof, de Valera received a rousing welcome at a reception organised by the Friends of Irish Freedom, where Judge Cohalan enthusiastically introduced him, proclaiming, 'For the first time in Irish history we have the President of the Irish Republic on American soil.'[192]

De Valera's first public appearance made the front-page of the *New York Times* the next morning. Meeting reporters again that day, he expressed Ireland's desire for the closest possible commercial and political relationship with the United States. He announced that the elected government of the Irish Republic would send accredited representatives to the Paris Peace Conference and ambassadors and consuls to other countries.

The American newspapers knew little about him beyond his role as the revolutionary Sinn Féin leader. They reported that he had been sentenced to be shot in 1916, saved only by 'his American citizenship'; had been imprisoned as part of a German Plot in Ireland while America was at war with Germany; elected to the British parliament while in prison and had escaped story-book style from Lincoln Jail just four months earlier. The mysterious ease with which he had eluded the British since his escape added to his popular interest.[193] Reporters eventually dug up details on his life, learning that he had been born in New York thirty-six years earlier:

> His father was a Spanish-American, his mother an Irish woman. When de Valera was two years old his father died and the family re-moved to Ireland [*sic*], where the boy was educated. He held the Professorship of Mathematics at several colleges in Dublin at different times, then became active in the free Ireland movement.[194]

Critics of his presence in America and those concerned about border controls wanted to know how he managed to enter the United States. He mischievously suggested that he might have come by air. Nine days earlier, Alcock and Brown had taken off from Newfoundland and sixteen hours later had landed safely in Clifden, completing the first non-stop transatlantic flight. A story doing the rounds was that he had stepped onto a seaplane in front of unsuspecting British officers, flown to a waiting yacht, and that another seaplane met him off the coast of New York.

De Valera had also come to America to raise money. 'It is obvious that the work of our Government cannot be carried on without funds,' he told reporters on 25 June.[195] The Irish parliament had approved a plan to raise a bond of £500,000, with £250,000 to be raised in Ireland and the other £250,000 ($1.25 million) offered for subscription in America. The Irish President denied 'most emphatically' that Russian or German money had ever been used to finance the Sinn Féin movement.[196]

Upon arriving in New York, de Valera raised the American bond target to $10 million. However, due to mismanagement, the campaign only raised $5 million, still a considerable sum for the nascent Irish government. In Ireland, the funding campaign exceeded its target, despite being declared illegal and suppressed by Dublin Castle.

Meanwhile, reporters confirmed from official sources that de Valera would not be interfered with unless he violated American law, with officials at the State Department intimating that if the object of the money was to create or equip a military force it would make him liable under the Neutrality Act.[197] When asked by reporters, Senator Lusk, chairman of the committee investigating Bolshevism and other seditious activities, stated that he was 'quite sure that De Valera's activities do not come within the purview of the committee's work'.

The *New York Times* published a scathing editorial criticising the Irish Republic, the bond funding and alleged links to radicals, and interpreted de Valera's comments as being pro-German:

> Many thousands of Irishmen – men like Tom Kettle and William Redmond [Home Rule supporters] – were dying for the freedom of the world; and for the sake of the memory of those men, if for no other reason, justice is due to Ireland. But where was the Irish Republic?[198]
>
> … it was a little tactless of Professor De Valera to tell us how much better off Ireland would have been under the rule of 'Kaiser, Emperor, or Czar'. It is six months since fighting ceased, but the Kaiser is not yet a popular hero in this country. Our distinguished visitor has hitched his wagon to a fallen star.

The newspaper incorrectly reported that Soviet Russia, through its 'intensively investigated' envoy Ludwig Martens, had recognised the Irish Republic. While de Valera favoured seeking recognition from the Soviet government, he was overruled by the cabinet in Dublin.[199] The following year, Irish envoys in New York gave a $20,000 loan to the Russian government, accepting jewels valued at $25,000 as collateral.[200] The jewels were restored to the Russian government in 1949 after repayment of the original loan.

One week before de Valera docked in New York, the US Senate passed a resolution expressing sympathy for the aspirations of the Irish people for a government of its own choice. The resolution, passed by a majority of sixty to one, had been carefully crafted and deftly steered through Senate committees by Cohalan and the Friends of Irish Freedom. Though the resolution had been diluted in committee from full recognition of the Irish Republic, its passage marked another step, and an important one, on the path of recognition. By this time, the Friends of Irish Freedom had evolved into a powerful lobbying organisation with offices in New York and Washington.[201]

De Valera believed that he could compel the United States government to officially recognise the Irish Republic by harnessing the power of public opinion. Official recognition, however, was not a realistic goal in the timeframe he envisioned. Pro-English sentiment in the White House and Congress was too strong. Even the English understood that the Senate resolution was largely symbolic, as revealed in a secret communication. 'Several of the Senators, Republicans and Democrats, with whom I talked,' reported Sir William Wiseman, a British intelligence officer in New York, 'admit that they do not regard a separate Irish Republic as either feasible or desirable, and all they meant by the resolution was to register their conviction that something ought to be done.'[202]

The Friends of Irish Freedom calculated that 'a mere fraction' of the loosely estimated twenty million Americans with Irish blood had given a thought to Ireland.[203] To address this, the group had already launched a nationwide education and propaganda campaign to raise awareness of the Irish struggle for independence, and to elevate the status of the Irish Race in American society, a core part of its mandate.

De Valera realised too late that recognition by the United States government could only be achieved by demonstrating that an independent Ireland was in America's own geopolitical interest. Appearing before a Senate Foreign Relations Committee, Cohalan had argued that it was in America's commercial and military interest that an independent Ireland, instead of England, controlled the Irish deep-water ports. The British Empire, which still held considerable naval superiority over the United States, had used that advantage against trade rivals in the past, as the Dutch, French and Spanish had learned to their cost. 'England cannot continue to control the world unless she controls the sea,' Cohalan told the Senate committee, '[and] her continued control of the sea is dependent on her continued control of Ireland'.[204]

During the final throes of Scott's three-week bender, he took a train to Boston to visit Stephan Parrott, a Newman and Princeton classmate, who had also been adopted by Father Fay as one of his spiritual sons. Scott's ledger entry for June shows his activity during the month: Charles 'Sap' Donahoe visited New York and they had a 'big party', he travelled to Montgomery and Zelda broke off the engagement and he journeyed to Boston to meet Parrot and continued to booze: 'Sap arrives. Big party. Montgomery. The break. Drunk in N.Y. Boston with Stephen Parrot …'[205]

On 29 June, when Scott was in Boston, de Valera basked in the adulation of a vast crowd of at least 50,000 people packed into Fenway Park, home of the Red Sox.[206] Newsreel footage captured de Valera waving his Panama hat, his face alight, smiling and nodding, mouthing acknowledgements of his welcome. A sea of hats filled the playing field, along with American flags, tricolours and banners in support of Irish freedom.[207] De Valera initially declined the invitation to speak – he did not want to do a speaking tour of the country – but was persuaded otherwise by Cohalan. The meeting was a monster propaganda success. According to John Devoy in the *Gaelic American*, the New York papers gave de Valera 'more space than they have given to anything Irish for many years and were much fairer than is their habit'.[208] During an automobile tour of Boston and Cambridge, de Valera laid wreaths at the elm tree under which Washington reputedly took command of the American revolutionary army, at the Minute Man statue in Lexington and at Bunker Hill, in tribute to the men of Irish blood who fought there.[209]

When Scott returned to New York and then left for St Paul on 4 July, authorities were on high alert for threatened Bolshevik, anarchist and other 'red flag' violence.[210] Two days earlier, the *New York Times* published a cable from Switzerland suggesting collusion and cooperation between de Valera and Russian Bolshevists and German propagandists.[211] Once back in St Paul, Scott could not escape the intense media coverage of de Valera's visit, one Minnesota newspaper reporting that 'these United States are becoming "all het up" over the Irish question'.[212] Inspired by the reaction to de Valera's presence in the country, he added a new scene to *This Side of Paradise*.

In the scene, Amory Blaine seeks the company of Mrs. Lawrence who was modelled on the influential Margaret 'Daisy' Chanler, whose circle of friends included Father Fay, Henry Adams and Theodore Roosevelt.[213] She had married Major Winthrop Chanler, a 'Rough Rider' alongside Roosevelt during the Spanish-American War and latterly an aide to General Pershing, commander of the American Expeditionary Forces. Father Fay had introduced Scott to Mrs Chanler and he became friendly with her son Teddy, an author, composer and godson of Roosevelt.

Amory Blaine telephones Mrs Lawrence who informs him that she thinks Monsignor Darcy (Father Fay) is in Boston. She invites him to take lunch with her:

> 'I thought I'd better catch up, Mrs. Lawrence,' he said rather ambiguously when he arrived.

'Monsignor was here just last week,' said Mrs. Lawrence regretfully. 'He was very anxious to see you, but he'd left your address at home.'

'Did he think I'd plunged into Bolshevism?' asked Amory, interested.

'Oh, he's having a frightful time.'

'Why?'

'About the Irish Republic. He thinks it lacks dignity.'

'So?'

Mrs Lawrence explains the Monsignor's concerns;

'He went to Boston when the Irish President arrived and he was greatly distressed because the receiving committee, when they rode in an automobile, *would* [FSF italics] put their arms around the President.'

'I don't blame him.'

Amory finds great relief in being away from stifling New York and in the company of a woman of 'perfect grace and dignity'. He confides in her his search for meaning and connection. When he leaves Mrs Lawrence, Amory walks away with a feeling of satisfaction.

It was amusing to discuss again such subjects as … the Irish Republic …

> There seemed suddenly to be much left in life, if only this
> revival of old interests did not mean that he was backing away
> from it again – backing away from life itself.

This scene was written contemporaneously with de Valera's first weeks in America and held personal significance for the writer because it was Scott, not Father Fay, who had seen de Valera in the automobile in Boston. The priest had died six months earlier.

That the Irish Republic, personified in de Valera, lacked 'dignity' hinted at the commonly held view that the Irish people were unfit to govern themselves. John Quinn, an Irish-American lawyer, patron of Irish arts, supporter of Home Rule and friend of Shane Leslie believed that the men who would go into the Home Rule parliament 'would be of a different breed and kind than those who have gone into the Dublin municipal corporation'.

Leslie and his ilk had failed to see the rise of the new leaders, few of whom had been active in politics before 1916, and did not grasp the importance the new generation attached to economic freedom, as well as to political freedom, which Home Rule would not deliver. He believed, incorrectly, that 'nobody cared a straw for free trade or taxes, for home or foreign policy'.[214] In contrast, Michael Collins, the young Minister for Finance, issued a press statement for release in America one month before *This Side of Paradise* was published:

The enemy government quickly realised that the economic policy of the Dáil [Irish parliament] was as great a danger to them as its political policy, that in fact the elected Government of Ireland stood for social and economical deliverance, no less than for political deliverance.

Completely disillusioned with politics, Leslie wrote to Joe Tumulty, President Wilson's private secretary:

For three years I have done my utmost to retain Irish confidence in the President but English policy gives me no choice between Sinn Féin and becoming an American. Could you enable me to enlist in the American forces now engaged in Russia or Siberia?[215]

Rancid Accusations

'Between the rancid accusations of Edward Carson and
Justice Cohalan, [Amory] had completely tired of the Irish
question; yet there had been a time when his own Celtic traits
were pillars of his personal philosophy.'

F. Scott Fitzgerald, *This Side of Paradise*

On 12 July 1919, Edward Carson, the fiery leader of
the Ulster Unionist Party, rose to his feet in front
of a mass demonstration outside Belfast. An imposing
figure with the oratory skills of a barrister and ready wit,
he exclaimed before the enthusiastic crowd that there
were only two choices available in Ireland: to maintain
the Union with the United Kingdom and loyalty to the
King, or – to mocking laughter from the crowd – 'an
Irish Republic, with your hats off to the President, Mr. de
Valera, who is now working against you in America'.[216]
Carson ridiculed those wanting to be citizens of a 'little
nation, a nation great in itself, but, after all, much greater
as part of an Empire'.

He warned that the Protestant people of the North of
Ireland would resist by force of arms if any of their rights
as British citizens were taken away. Carson also had a

special message for those across the Atlantic supporting the Irish Republic:

There was a campaign going on in America, at the present moment, fostered by the Catholic Church there with great funds at their disposal, which would be soon joined by the Germans and their funds in order to create great anti-British feeling …

Heaven knows, I want good feeling between America and this country. I believe that the whole future of the world probably depends on the relations between the United States of America and ourselves, but I am not going to submit to this kind of a campaign, whether for that friendship or for any other purpose.

I today seriously say to America,

'You attend to your own affairs; we will attend to ours. You look after your own questions at home, and we will look after ours. We will brook no interference in our own affairs by any country, however powerful.'

Carson was particularly piqued by the recent visit of the American Commission on Irish Independence to Ireland. The commission, set up to give authority to the work of three high-profile Irish-Americans attending the Paris Peace Conference, was funded by the Friends of Irish Freedom:

> To obtain for the delegates selected by the people of Ireland a
> hearing before the Peace Conference and to place before the
> Conference, if this hearing is not given, the case of Ireland,
> her insistence on her right to self-determination and to inter-
> national recognition of the republican form of government
> established by her people.[217]

The commission chairman, Frank P. Walsh, a well-known labour attorney and former pacifist, had been appointed joint chairman of the National War Labour Board and chairman of the Industrial Relations Commission by President Wilson. Walsh was accompanied by Edward Dunne, former governor of Illinois and mayor of Chicago, and Michael J. Ryan, a banker and lawyer, and former Home Rule supporter.

The commission failed to obtain a hearing at the peace conference for a delegation from Ireland, but it generated significant publicity for the Irish Republic when the commissioners made a ten-day visit to Ireland, after reluctantly receiving permission from the British government. They addressed the third session of Dáil Éireann, the counter-state parliament, held at the residence of the nationalist Lord Mayor of Dublin. After the meeting, military and police gathered in front of the building ostensibly looking for escaped convicts. The following day the commission was denied permission to visit Mountjoy prison, before showing diplomatic visas and convincing the authorities that prime minister Lloyd George had urged them to investigate conditions in Ireland for themselves. On the next day they were refused permission to enter the military district in Mayo and turned back by soldiers.[218]

During the tour the commission members publicly expressed the need for Irish independence, the failures of British rule in the country and the support of the American people for the Irish cause. Lloyd George complained to Colonel House, President Wilson's chief adviser: 'I now find these gentlemen, so far from investigating the Irish problem in a spirit of impartiality, announced on arrival in Dublin that they had come there to forward the disruption of the United Kingdom, and the establishment of Ireland as an independent Republic.'[219] The outbursts in Ireland lost the commission the support of Colonel House and the official American delegation.

Walsh's experience in Paris turned him against President Wilson and the League of Nations; he described the plenary session of the peace conference as akin to 'mob primaries out in Missouri'.[220] His lack of political diplomacy led to the mission ending in controversy. A meeting with President Wilson, arranged just three weeks before his return to America, turned into a provocative and tetchy encounter, with both sides issuing threats. Walsh succeeded, not for the first time, in getting under the skin of the man for whom he had once campaigned. During the meeting, he warned that unless some relief was given to Ireland, 'workers there would have, in self defence, to set up Soviet governments or do something else to relieve the situation'.[221]

Wilson responded by explaining that no small nation could appear before the peace conference unless there was unanimous consent from the committee of four, which would not be forthcoming since the conference only considered nations actually concerned in the war. As one American plenipotentiary put it, Irish affairs had 'nothing to do with making peace with Germany and Austria'.[222] Walsh then quoted Wilson's own self-determination principles back at him, angering the president who, forgetting himself, shouted that he 'didn't give a damn'.[223]

A slip-up by Walsh before the Republican-controlled Senate Foreign Relations Committee resulted in the release of the full transcript of the meeting to the press – much of it politically sensitive to the president. Walsh had indicated to the committee that he would submit his Paris interviews in private 'because they might prove embarrassing to some gentlemen'. Republican senators, seeing an opportunity to embarrass the president, voted to receive the interviews only as part of the public record.[224]

The cooling of the relationship between Walsh and Wilson had begun earlier in the year. During a brief return to America, the president reluctantly agreed to meet a delegation of Irish-American leaders. His only stipulation was that Cohalan, who had opposed him within the Democratic party, could not be part of the delegation, resulting in Walsh taking the lead. After the meeting, the president complained to colleagues, 'They were so insistent … I had hard work keeping my temper.'[225] His first impulse was to tell them to 'go to hell'.[226]

Edward Carson responded to the actions and proclamations of Walsh during his speech in Belfast:

What right had an American mission to come to this country – come here in a breach of hospitality of one nation toward another – to attempt to stir up strife in matters in which they were not connected?

The encouragement those men gave the Sinn Fein Party has created for the British Government far more difficulties than they ever had before.

Over 3,500 miles away, across an ocean and half a continent, Scott read Carson's speech, which had made the front page of the *New York Times* and was syndicated nationwide under the headline: 'Carson Rebukes America for Irish Agitation, "Attend to Your Own Affairs," Ulster Chief Warns'.[227]

Scott was incensed by Carson's bitter attack towards the end of his speech on Sir Horace Plunkett, a Home Rule supporter and friend of Shane Leslie. Plunkett, from an Anglo-Irish Protestant background and educated at Eton and Oxford, was a pioneer of the agricultural cooperative movement in Ireland. Two weeks before Carson's speech, Plunkett had launched the Irish Dominion League to promote a new form of Home Rule. The *New*

York Times reported on the development with the headline, 'Island Under Plunkett Scheme Would Be Virtually a Republic'.[228]

Plunkett had travelled to America at the beginning of the year spending considerable time with Leslie and Bourke Cockran. Leslie mentioned Plunkett in his books *The End of a Chapter* and *The Irish Issue in its American Aspect*. In the aftermath of Father Fay's death, he had written to Scott: 'Cheer up and come and see me when you are in N.Y. I hope to be here a few more weeks while Horace Plunkett is in the country.'[229]

Plunkett proposed that Ireland would have a parliament in Dublin with full control over internal affairs and would join the League of Nations, while remaining part of the British Empire. Naval and military defence would remain under the control of the British government. Plunkett pointed out the danger to Irish products if Ireland were a republic severed from the British Empire. The right of minorities, particularly the Protestant population in the north east, would be constitutionally recognised. The group's manifesto was signed by well-known Home Rulers, some Unionists, forty-five Irish peers and baronets, privy councillors, bank and railway directors, and lawyers.

The majority of Unionists opposed the scheme, preferring to maintain the existing constitutional arrangement of the United Kingdom of Great Britain and Ireland. Sinn Fein, the largest political party, rejected the proposal because Britain would retain control of income tax, customs and excise, monetary policy and banking regulation, as well as military, foreign affairs, navigation and all communication links, and the king would remain as head of state.

The Friends of Irish Freedom called the founding of the Irish Dominion League a 'panic stricken effort on the part of the Tory element in England to fend off an Irish Republic. It is what England would have offered to Washington in 1776 – if her statesmen could have foreseen the outcome of the American struggle.'[230] Cohalan pointedly said of Horace Plunkett that he was 'a good man but always 3 laps behind'.[231]

Plunkett's comment on the potential threat to Irish trade if the country left the British Empire was economically naïve. England already controlled Ireland's imports and exports by forcing all trade through her ports. The Act of Union in 1800 and the merger of the Irish and British exchequers in 1817 had made Ireland politically, administratively and fiscally part of the United Kingdom of Great Britain and Ireland. From January 1817, the exchequer of the United Kingdom received the tax revenues of Ireland and paid for its capital and administrative costs.[232] Cohalan, appearing before the Senate Foreign Relations Committee, noted that over-taxation on Ireland amounted to $1.7 billion over twenty years.[233]

Ireland was living with the consequences of British economic policy over the previous century. Although the country had a vibrant banking sector, domestic banks invested the savings of the Irish people in short-term investments in financial institutions in London and in British government bonds. Irish banks withheld substantial loans from Irish traders, entrepreneurs and private individuals. Irish industry was deliberately starved of financial capital. Ireland did not industrialise, instead becoming a market for easily accessible British manufactured goods. Irish tenants had been cleared from the land to produce cattle and grain. Ireland turned into a corn basket and cattle ranch for England, which could not feed its rapidly expanding population.

The easily grown and nutritious potato became the staple food for the Irish peasantry, allowing most of Ireland's grain to be exported. The financial, industrial and agricultural policies imposed on Ireland perpetually bound the Irish people to a miserable existence, dependent on a single crop, with limited access to education and advancement, and resulting rapid population growth. This was a recipe for disaster if the potato crop failed, which it did in 1845. Diseased with blight, it rotted in the ground. Famine caused 100,000 deaths across Europe, but Ireland's suffering was biblical in scale.

Vast initial relief measures were replaced by a laissez-faire economic doctrine; famine would reduce the population to a sustainable level. Many in the English establishment, and in the Irish Protestant Ascendancy, believed that the population decline was divine providence. Charles Trevelyan, in charge of the government's response to the catastrophe, wrote, 'The judgment of God sent the calamity to teach the Irish a lesson, that calamity must not be too much mitigated …The real evil with which we have to contend is not the physical evil of the Famine, but the moral evil of the selfish, perverse and turbulent character of the people.[234] However, many ordinary English people were sympathetic to the Irish situation sending substantial aid to the country. Others around the world were also sympathetic. The Choctaw nation, the first tribe to be relocated during the Trail of Tears, sent $170 for hunger relief.

Under the political and economic union with Great Britain, the population of Ireland was halved between 1840 and 1900, from 8 million to 4 million people. The policy of depopulation continued into the twentieth-century. Viscount French, appointed Lord Lieutenant of Ireland in 1918, blamed the troubled situation in the country on the absence of emigration during the war years, stating in an interview: 'The principal cause of the trouble is that for five years emigration has practically stopped. In this country there are from one hundred thousand to two hundred thousand young men from eighteen to twenty five years of age who in normal times would have emigrated.'[235]

The new native government, suppressed and forced underground, developed its own plans to counter the structural weaknesses in the economy. To relieve the shortage of capital, Michael Collins, the Minister for Finance, set-up a commercial bank using a dummy corporation to disguise its ownership from the Dublin Castle administration.

During his speech in Belfast, Edward Carson called Sir Horace Plunkett a 'lundy', a byword for traitor among Unionists, declaring that he was 'thoroughly hated and distrusted by both sides'. He suggested that Plunkett 'ought to join the Sinn Feiners. Those are his real colours for the moment.' Plunket noted in his diary, 'Carson ... made a violent attack on the Irish Dominion League & on me personally ... It was a vulgar performance ...'[236]

Horace Plunkett was uncle to Edward Drax Plunkett, 18th Baron of Dunsany. More commonly known as Lord Dunsany, the Anglo-Irish fantasy writer and dramatist was popular in New York in 1919.[237] The *New York Times* favourably reviewed his plays, *The Laughter of the Gods* and *The Murderers*. Scott incorporated Dunsany in *This Side of Paradise*:

> One day Tom [D'Invilliers] and Amory tried reciting their own and Lord Dunsany's poems to the music of Kerry's graphophone.
>
> 'Chant!' cried Tom. 'Don't recite! Chant!'
>
> Amory, who was performing, looked annoyed, and claimed that he needed a record with less piano in it. Kerry [another friend] thereupon rolled on the floor in stifled laughter.
>
> 'Put on "Hearts and Flowers"!' he howled. 'Oh, my Lord, I'm going to cast a kitten.'
>
> 'Shut off the damn graphophone,' Amory cried, rather red in the face. 'I'm not giving an exhibition.'

Carson's direct attack on Sir Horace Plunkett and on Lord Dunsany by association pushed Scott further away from interest in Ireland and from his Celtic identity. In *This Side of Paradise*, he wrote: 'Between the rancid accusations of Edward Carson and Justice Cohalan, he had completely tired of the Irish question; yet there had been a time when his own Celtic traits were pillars of his personal philosophy.'

But Scott's antagonism towards Cohalan had deeper roots than the trans-Atlantic political spat.

STIGMA

'Because of our Irish blood, we are handicapped in America and, consequently, have an interest in the freedom of the race.'

Justice Daniel F. Cohalan

The Irish-American experience of Daniel Cohalan differed significantly from that of the younger Scott. As a child in New York State during the late 1860s and early 1870s, the future justice of the New York Supreme Court witnessed his father fighting sectarian and racial bigotry while supporting Irish nationalist and cultural causes. Unlike in St Paul, nativist mobs in the east had destroyed Irish homes and torched Catholic churches.

Cohalan refused to accept that his American identity was inferior to that of Anglo-Americans. Confident in both his Americanism and Irish heritage, he devoted his life to elevating the status of the Irish in America. As one of the founding members of the American Irish Historical Society in 1897, he worked to raise awareness of Irish accomplishments and to counter revisionist pro-English interpretations of American history.

Cohalan chaired the third Irish Race Convention, which authorised the raising of $1 million through an Irish Victory Fund. One of the fund's aims was to counter English propaganda that misrepresented American history.[238] The Friends of Irish Freedom published letters and pamphlets highlighting the Irish contribution to America's success. They sent a letter to Senator John Sharp Williams, the only senate member to vote against an expression of sympathy for the aspirations of the Irish people, pointing out that at least 38 per cent of the American revolutionary army was of Irish birth or descent.[239]

In contrast to Scott, who supported the existence of a governing class, Cohalan opposed the ever-closer relations developing between the Anglo-American elite and their English counterparts.[240] In Scott's eyes, Cohalan was one of the 'muckers' within American politics. Scott voiced his disillusionment with the political system, and his identity aspirations, when Amory Blaine admitted, 'Sometimes I wish I'd been an Englishman.'

Cohalan's grandfather, a widower, emigrated from Ireland in 1848 with three daughters and his twelve-year-old son, Cohalan's father. The latter became a stone mason and later established a successful glass business.[241] Educated at Catholic Manhattan College, Cohalan played on the baseball team that defeated Yale, the college that Princeton-educated Scott 'wouldn't have gone … for a million'.[242] Cohalan likely took great pleasure in that victory, since a Princeton or Yale education was not an option for him. He had American revolutionary roots through a great-grandfather, Captain Eugene McCarthy, who had reportedly served as aide-de-camp to the Marquis de Lafayette during the American Revolutionary War, after which he had returned to Ireland.[243]

Admitted to the New York Bar in 1888, and without the advantage of an Anglo heritage or an Ivy League education, his path to success came through the Tammany machine, a counter-weight to WASP[244] influence in New York politics. Cohalan joined the Democratic party, drafting state party platforms and serving as a delegate to national conventions. As a grand sachem of Tammany Hall, he had been a trusted adviser of Boss Charles F. Murphy. After narrowly missing the nomination for state senator, he was appointed a justice of the New York Supreme Court in 1911 to fill an unexpired term, and later that year was elected in his own right. In 1916, he co-founded the Friends of Irish Freedom, while also being a member of Clan-na-Gael, which had financed and helped plan the 1916 Easter Rising.

Passionate about Ireland, Cohalan owned a house in Cork and frequently visited before the war. Naturally, he supported the Irish cause. However, he fought for Irish independence – risking reputation, career and even freedom – as an American 'first, last and all the time'. He believed that as long as the homeland was under English rule a stigma attached to the Irish race. 'Because of our Irish blood,' he wrote, 'we are handicapped in America and, consequently, have an interest in the freedom of the race.'[245] The establishment of an independent Irish state with its people free from English colonial rule and Ireland taking her place among the nation states of Europe was crucial to the elevation of the Irish race in America.

Cohalan nurtured cross-party political support for Ireland in Washington, where he spent many weekends. 'I was exhausted when the time came for him to board the train for New York,' recalled the head of the Irish National Bureau, 'after outplaying the British Embassy at their own game of "secret diplomacy".'[246] His detailed preparation and breadth of knowledge was evident during a Senate hearing. One moment, he debated congressional powers of recognition for new nations; the next, he detailed the conditions prevailing in Ireland, from the 1918 election to the formation of Dáil Éireann, and the campaign of repression against the civilian arms of the counter-state government, concluding by demonstrating the strategic benefit of Irish independence to America.

Cohalan opposed the League of Nations viewing it as an infringement on the sovereignty of America and a cover for a special alliance with England. This view placed him at odds with Shane Leslie, who had promoted a formal alliance between England and America in *The Celt and the World*. Cohalan supported the formation of a real League of Nations that 'will include all peoples, great or small, that … will be a step in the direction of the brotherhood of man'.[247] He believed that the 'English made' League enhanced the imperial ambitions of Britain and Japan, posing a threat to America – a view shared by many at the time.

Both Democratic and Republican law makers were troubled by the terms of the agreement establishing the League of Nations. Many believed that President Wilson had failed to deliver on his pre-war promises, caving to the demands of Britain, France and Japan – the three surviving post-war empires, each of which had added to their territories under the mandate system. David Lloyd George, so pleased with his own performance at the Paris Peace Conference, quipped that he had done well, considering he 'was seated between Jesus Christ and Napoleon' – a reference to the idealistic Wilson, striving to fashion a new world order, and the pragmatic Clemenceau, French prime minister, determined to achieve total victory over Germany.

President Wilson's refusal to bring senior Republicans to Paris had been a strategic mistake. Republicans had taken control of the Senate and a two-thirds majority was required to pass the League of Nations covenant. The terms of the covenant posed a direct challenge to the constitutional core of America, a country barely a century and a half old, and still within living memory of its civil war. Ratifying the agreement would mean abandoning the doctrine of avoiding permanent alliances with countries of the Old World and could be seen to override the Monroe Doctrine, an anchor of American security considerations since the early 1800s.

Britain had successfully negotiated individual voting rights for each of its dominions, including Australia and Canada, giving the British Empire six votes in the League compared to just one vote for the United States. A particularly thorny issue was Article 10 of the covenant, which placed an obligation on America to deploy its military to preserve the 'territorial integrity' of any League member. Under the US Constitution, only Congress had the authority to declare war and authorise the deployment of military forces overseas.

Article 10 of the covenant also presented a new obstacle to Irish independence by obliging all members to protect the territorial integrity of the United Kingdom. Cohalan explained to a Senate hearing that if 'a League of Nations had been in existence at the time of the American Revolution, France could not have come to the assistance of the Thirteen Colonies'. He added that America would be compelled to send her military into Ireland 'not for the purpose of helping them in their struggle but in order to help England to rivet the chains upon her'.

The Friends of Irish Freedom and the British government fought an intensive propaganda battle during the Senate debates on the League of Nations. Philip Gibbs, a former English war correspondent, called the Irish campaign 'elaborate, widespread and brilliantly organized'.[248] Lord Northcliffe, the owner of *The Times*, warned that those trained in the arts of swaying public opinion were urgently needed in America.[249]

In *This Side of Paradise*, Scott defended President Wilson and the League of Nations against 'quarter-educated, stale-minded men'; one time, they call the president 'just a dreamer, not practical'; then, 'rail at him for making his dreams realities'. Scott also opposed Cohalan's stance against America entering the war on the side of England, writing that Amory Blaine believed Germany stood for 'everything repugnant to him; for materialism and the direction of tremendous licentious force'.

On the same day that Edward Carson spoke in Belfast, the Orangemen's Association of the United States marched through New York to mark the 300th anniversary of the Battle of the Boyne. The historic battle resulted in the defeat of the exiled Catholic King James II by the army of Protestant King William III, known as William of Orange, and was instrumental in ensuring the ascendency of Anglican Protestantism in Ireland. The chief speaker at the dinner following the parade, former Supreme Grand Master Henry Stewart, declared: 'We are going to tell Bourke Cockran and Justice Cohalan that, as long as Great Britain has a gun and a man to stand behind the gun, Ireland will never get the independence they seek.'[250]

Cohalan spoke to a reporter from the *New York Times* the following day:

> While the gallant Sir Edward Carson was attempting to stir up religious strife in Belfast yesterday, his cohorts in New York were making a desperate effort along the same line, and while Carson contented himself with ordering the future policy of America, the New York element denounced American citizens for daring to assist a nation in its desperate struggle for liberty.

Sir Edward Carson forgets that America won the war and has therefore a right to dictate terms of peace. He forgets, too, that when we entered the war, which was won by the strength, vigor, and courage of America, we did so on grounds which pledge us to bring to the oppressed peoples of the earth the right of self-determination.

When the President of the United States laid down his celebrated Fourteen Points he made no condition or qualification as to the peoples to whom the right of self-determination was to be applied, and the great mass of the people of America believed that it was to apply to those nations which groaned under the tyranny of England as well as to those that suffered under the tyranny of the Central Powers.[251]

This response to Carson, hardly unexpected, did not warrant Scott's characterisation as a 'rancid' accusation. While Scott's strong reaction to the Ulster leader was rooted in his attack on Horace Plunkett, his antipathy towards Cohalan lay in their different perceptions of self-worth. Polar opposite views on governance in America, and on the Irish question and on the League of Nations reflected their divergent attitudes to their ethnic identity, one proudly fighting for the elevation of the Irish race in America; the other trying to escape it.

'BUT I HAVEN'T ANY PEOPLE'

Following the successful 1922 publication of his second novel, *The Beautiful and Damned*, Scott was invited by Bunny Wilson, now a critic and journalist for the influential *The Bookman*, to feature in a literary spotlight. In the novel, a young artist Anthony Patch and his flapper wife Gloria Gilbert, characters modelled on Scott and Zelda, party to excess, fall victim to dissipation and ruin their lives during the dawn of the Jazz Age. Eager to be viewed as a serious writer beyond his reputation as the philosopher of the flapper, which had been reinforced by similar themes in his published short-stories, Scott agreed to the spotlight. However, accepting the invitation came with risk. The prickly Wilson, though a friend, wouldn't hesitate to write a takedown piece.

Scott featured no Irish-American protagonists in *The Beautiful and Damned*, not even Anthony Patch based on himself, but he did include a number of negative Irish cameos. Patch has an affair with Geraldine Burke because he is 'wary of girls of his own class'. He tells her an allegorical tale of the aristocratic Chevalier O'Keefe exiled in France, an 'Irishman – the wild sort with a genteel brogue' and 'reddish hair' whose downfall is caused by association with a peasant girl. He writes of Irish girls 'casting their eyes, with license at last to do so, upon a society of young Tammany politicians, pious undertakers, and grown-up choirboys'. When Patch's English servant enlists in the British Army, he hires 'a gaunt, big-boned Irishwoman' whom Gloria 'loathed because she discussed the glories of Sinn Fein as she served breakfast'. Scott also included a caricature of a 'greedy Mick', an awkward bank manager named Halloran.

When he received a draft of *The Bookman* spotlight for his review, Scott was disappointed and worried. While Wilson's piece was insightful, it painted him as an intellectual lightweight and faint praise came punctured with caveats.

> For he has been given imagination without intellectual control of it; he has been given a desire for beauty without an esthetic ideal; and he has been given a gift for expression without many ideas to express.
>
> Consider, for example, the novel, with which he founded his reputation, 'This Side of Paradise'. It has almost every fault and deficiency that a novel can possibly have …
>
> … it was well written – well written in spite of everything …
>
> He has an instinct for graceful and vivid prose which some of his more serious fellows might envy.[252]

Wilson cited three influences on Scott's writing – the Midwest, his Irish heritage and liquor. He recommended that he should write more about the Midwest, the 'only milieu that he thoroughly understands'. He criticised his approach to the east bringing 'to it the standards of the wealthy west – the preoccupation with display, the love of magnificence and jazz, the vigorous social atmosphere of amiable flappers and youths comparatively unpoisoned as yet by the snobbery of the east'.

The draft spotlight created a tactical dilemma for Scott. He needed to persuade Wilson to remove the Irish and liquor influences and to tone down the intellectual criticism, without risking his crotchety friend pulling the spotlight entirely. He adopted an obsequious tone in his reply to Wilson: 'I don't see how I could possibly be offended at anything in it … Of course, I'm going to carp at it a little but merely to conform to convention.'[253]

The liquor influence was his most serious problem. While acknowledging his 'dope-fiend' reputation, he pleaded with Wilson to take it out because it 'would hurt me more than you could imagine'. He believed it would expose him to attacks by moralists, hurt his relations with relatives, in particular Zelda's parents, and respectable friends, and 'much more important, financially'. His approach to removing the Irish influence was more delicate, pointing out that 'incidently, though it doesn't matter, I'm not Irish on Father's side – that's where Francis Scott Key comes in'. So concerned was he with the liquor reference, he backed down on the removal of the Irish influence.

He had previously downplayed his Irishness to Wilson when he sent a mock family tree to him. The genealogical fiction traced his ancestry to various nobles including Mary, Queen of Scots, Lord Edward Fitzgerald, Sir Walter Scott, Duke Fitzgerald, the Earl of Leinster and Francis Scott Key. The family branch ended with: 'F. Scott Fitzgerald (drunkard).'[254]

To his relief, Wilson cut the liquor influence in the spotlight. However, he described his friend as 'Irish on both sides'. He attached stereotypical Irish traits to him and his literary work. Scott is 'amusing and clever … rather child-like … like a woman, he is not given to abstract or impersonal thought … an actor in an elfin harlequinade'. Wilson's characterisation as Irish 'on both sides' hinted that he was not a true American of Anglo-Saxon heritage.

> … he brings to the writing of fiction some qualities rarely found in America. For, like the Irish, he is romantic, but is also cynical about romance; he is ecstatic and bitter; lyrical and sharp. He is bound to represent himself as a Playboy, yet he mocks incessantly at the Playboy. He is vain, a little malicious, of quick intelligence and wit and with a gift for turning language into something iridescent and magical.[255]

Wilson takes a quote from Shaw's *John Bull's Other Island* to make a contrast between Irish imagination and fondness for alcohol and Anglo-Saxon form and structure: 'imagination, imagination, imagination; and imagination's such a torture that you can't bear it without whisky'.[256] Wilson was not alone in seeing Scott as Irish on both sides. One evening, he arrived home late after a drinking session, an argument ensued and he threw a favourite vase of Zelda's into the fireplace. She retaliated by calling his father an Irish policeman. Scott slapped her hard across the face making her nose bleed.[257]

Two years after the publication of *This Side of Paradise*, his self-deception of not being Irish on both sides had been exposed publicly. Within the book, Scott had gone even further in his rejection of his ethnicity. For a brief period, under the influence of Fay and Leslie – and their views of Celtic racial equality, even superiority – he appeared to have overcome the shame in his Irish heritage. This Celtic period peaked in late 1918 when he received his embarkation orders. In the novel, Monsignor Darcy writes a letter to Amory Blaine as he was about to go to war; it is a flattering and egotistical missive from the father figure to the son.

> Of one thing I'm sure – Celtic you'll live and Celtic you'll die; so if you don't use heaven as a continual referendum for your ideas you'll find earth a continual recall to your ambitions.

… we're extraordinary, we're clever, we could be said, I suppose, to be brilliant. We can attract people, we can make atmosphere, we can almost lose our Celtic souls in Celtic subtleties, we can almost always have our own way …

The monsignor includes an Irish keen, or lament for the dead, written for his spiritual son, incorporated from a letter Scott had received from Father Fay. The keen features characters from Irish mythology and the early Irish church, including Aengus, symbolising youth, love and poetic inspiration and Cú Chulainn, the most famous of the Irish warrior heroes:

Ochone
He is gone from me the son of my mind
And he in his golden youth like Angus Oge
Angus of the bright birds
And his mind strong and subtle like the mind of Cuchulin on Muirtheme.

Scott's shame in his Irish ethnicity was too strong to overcome and, as the novel progressed, he writes cryptically that Amory Blaine is 'puzzled and depressed' by James Joyce's *A Portrait of the Artist as a Young Man*. His reason is only revealed in a letter to Wilson in 1922. Scott acquired a copy of *Ulysses* from the Brick Row Book Shop and wrote to Wilson after starting the novel: '… there is something about middle-class Ireland that depresses me inordinately – I mean gives me a sort of hollow, cheerless pain. Half of my ancestors came from just such an Irish strata or perhaps a lower one. The book makes me feel appallingly naked.'[258]

Scott was fascinated by Joyce. He selected *A Portrait of the Artist as a Young Man*, which, like his own debut novel, is an autobiographical coming of age story tracing the protagonist's growth to artistic maturity, as one of the ten best books he had read for a newspaper feature, predicting Joyce 'to be the most profound literary influence in the next fifty years'. He also chose *Nostromo*, by Joseph Conrad, which he considered the 'great novel of the past fifty years, as Ulysses is the great novel of the future'.[259]

By the end of *This Side of Paradise*, Amory rejects all his belief systems, including his Celtic pillars, when declaring: 'I know myself, but that is all.' But he also escapes his inherited ethnicity through a macabre wish fulfilment. Amory's father dies during his first year at Princeton. His mother dies just after the war. Scott's father and mother, Edward and Mollie, lived until 1931 and 1936 respectively. Though retaining her Irish ethnicity, Amory's mother is idealised as an elegant and refined version of Mollie McQuillan possessing 'exquisite' delicate features and 'consummate art and simplicity' in her style. With the convenient early death of his parents, Amory is liberated from his heritage.

'Amory,' she whispered, 'when you're ready for me I'll marry you.'

'We won't have much at first.'

'Don't!' she cried. 'It hurts when you reproach yourself for what you can't give me. I've got your precious self – and that's enough for me.'

'Tell me ...'

'You know, don't you? Oh, you know.'

'Yes, but I want to hear you say it.'

'I love you, Amory, with all my heart.'

'Always, will you?'

'All my life – Oh, Amory –'

'What?'

'I want to belong to you. I want your people to be my people. I want to have your babies.'

Amory replies:

'But I haven't any people.'

Part 2

Gatsby

THE VEGETABLE

'I have got myself into a terrible mess,' Fitzgerald wrote in desperation to Max Perkins on 7 November 1923.[260] At the end of his rope, he needed $650 in the bank within days or he would have to pawn his furniture. He did not dare meet Perkins in person. He already owed $3,500 to Scribner, but he pleaded with his friend, 'for God's sake try to fix it'. His play, *The Vegetable*, was due to open in ten days at the Nixon Apollo Theatre in Atlantic City. Feeling certain that the political satire would secure his financial future, he offered Perkins the first royalty payments until the full amount was cleared up. He told his patient editor a year earlier that the play would make him 'rich forever' and he would never have to bother him for money again.[261]

Fitzgerald had blown through substantial royalties received on two novels and two short story collections, *Flappers and Philosophers* and *Tales of the Jazz Age*, and had earned over $23,500 from movie rights to the novels and various short stories over the previous three years.[262] On seeing the film of *The Beautiful and Damned*, a despondent Fitzgerald complained, 'it's by far the worst movie I've ever seen in my life – cheap, vulgar, ill-constructed and shoddy'.[263] The film is lost and *This Side of Paradise* was never produced.

His get-rich-quick plan did not work; the opening night of his play was a disaster. 'It was a colossal frost,' Fitzgerald punned on the name of the protagonist Jerry Frost, the hen-pecked middle-class railway clerk with ambitions to become President of the United States. A fantasy dream scene in the second act proved too much for the gala audience, including Mayor Hylan of New York. Watching people leaving their seats and walking out, rustling their programmes and talking audibly in bored impatient whispers, Fitzgerald wanted to stop the show and say it was all a mistake.[264] During the second intermission, with his friend Ring Lardner, a sports columnist and short story writer, he asked the lead actor, 'Are you going to stay and do the last act?' He said he was. 'Don't be silly,' they laughed, 'we've met a bartender down the street who's an old friend of ours.'[265] That was the last he saw of them.

He had hoped the financial success of the play would provide breathing space to finish his third novel and free him from the misery of living pay cheque to pay cheque, or in his case, from short story to short story. A Model-T production line of stories, sold at good prices to *Cosmopolitan*, *Metropolitan* and *The Saturday Evening Post*, funded an extravagant lifestyle. Editors allowed him produce any story he wanted, so long as it was the same story in a different guise.

He had others to care for now. Zelda had resumed the engagement when Scribner agreed to publish *This Side of Paradise*. The couple married in the vestry of St Patrick's

Cathedral in New York in a small wedding in April 1920, attended by her three sisters and some friends. Neither set of parents was there. Frances Scott 'Scottie' Fitzgerald arrived eighteen months later. Emerging from the ether, Zelda remarked on her new-born girl, 'I hope it's beautiful and a fool – a beautiful little fool.'[266] Fitzgerald scribbled the words into his notebook.

During the summer before the debacle of *The Vegetable*, Scott had rented a house at 6 Gateway Drive on the Great Neck peninsula in Long Island. A short drive from Midtown Manhattan and with a good rail connection, Great Neck attracted a nouveau riche melange of media moguls, theatre stars, producers, musicians and the Hollywood-type before the movie industry moved to California. In a room over the garage, Fitzgerald began his novel 'retired into strict seclusion and celibacy', as Zelda regretfully remembered.[267]

Conjugal abstinence and seclusion did not last for long. His writing was interrupted by days and nights of 'constant drinking'.[268] He attended a party at the home of movie director Allen Dwan celebrating the completion of *Robin Hood*, his hit starring Douglas Fairbanks, and another party hosted by twenty-four-year-old actress Gloria Swanson attended by all the movie crowd. He threw a party for Zelda's popular sister Rosalind. His favourite pastime was drinking 'Oceans of Canadian ale' with Ring Lardner.[269]

Edmund Wilson wrote to a mutual friend in August that Fitzgerald was 'struggling with a new novel and very low in his mind'.[270] In a futile attempt at discipline, he made a new schedule of work in September.[271] When *The Vegetable* went into production the following month, putting the book aside he spent his days in the city at rehearsals and his nights making changes to the script.[272] He stopped writing short stories, straining his financial resources.

When the play flopped, he was humiliated and became depressed. His first literary failure heightened his insecurity, lowered his artistic confidence and placed him dangerously in debt. Fitzgerald mocked his precarious financial position in *How to Live on $36,000 a Year*, a piece penned for *The Saturday Evening Post*: 'I was $5,000 in debt, and my one idea was to get in touch with a reliable poorhouse where we could hire a room and bath for nothing a week.'[273] Though drained of money, he could take a single satisfaction from the experience: 'We had spent $36,000, and purchased for one year the right to be members of the newly rich class. What more can money buy?' His fear of poverty and desire for wealth were mockingly encapsulated in one story.

Fitzgerald had the ability to pull a rabbit out of a hat at his lowest points, as he had shown returning in despair to St Paul in 1919 to complete *This Side of Paradise*. On this occasion, he retreated to his damp bare room with an oil stove during a long and bitter winter, sometimes working through the night, to write eleven stories that earned him over $17,000. 'I've been sweating out trash since the failure of my play,' he reported to Thomas Boyd, a friend from St Paul.[274] With Fitzgerald's encouragement, Scribner had published Boyd's first novel, *Through the Wheat*, to critical success. Boyd's inscription on the copy he sent to his literary mentor described him as 'the most generous and engaging individual I've ever known – and without whom Saint Paul is a pretty sallow spot'.[275]

By April 1924 Fitzgerald was financially out of the woods. His health had suffered, but he was ready to go at the novel again. 'I really worked hard as hell last winter,' he confided to Perkins, '… it nearly broke my heart as well as my iron constitution.'[276] No longer willing to sacrifice his artistic credibility, he declared in another letter to his editor that his plan was to finish the novel in June, but with a caveat, 'you know how these things often work out. And even if it takes me 10 times that long I cannot let it go out unless it has the very best I'm capable of in it or even as I feel sometimes, something better than I'm capable of.'[277]

In the reflective letter, Fitzgerald regretted his dissipation and failure to deliver a new novel since he had completed *The Beautiful and Damned*. He had worked hard over the winter months, but during the two previous years he had written an average of just one hundred words a day, completing one play, half a dozen short stories and a small number of articles. 'If I'd spent this time reading or travelling or doing anything – even staying healthy – it'd be different,' he repented, 'but I spent it uselessly, neither in study nor in contemplation but only in drinking and raising hell generally.' He felt an 'enormous power' inside, if he could only harness it, but he had used up so much personal experience in the first two books that there was none left. His new novel had to be a 'purely creative work ... a consciously artistic achievement'. This worried him. 'I tread slowly and carefully,' he opened up to Perkins, 'and at times in considerable distress.'

'ABSOLUTION'

He had not fixed on a title for his novel. His preference was *Among Ash-Heaps and Millionaires*.[278] When the Long Island elite travelled by rail or on the main thoroughfare to New York, they passed by the unsightly Corona ash dump. Barges transported ash from coal-burning furnaces across the boroughs to Queens creating huge ash piles; one over 100 feet high was christened Mount Corona.[279] Scott wrote a vivid description of the ash dump, an important location and symbol in the novel.

> This is a valley of ashes – a fantastic farm where ashes grow like wheat into ridges and hills and grotesque gardens; where ashes take the forms of houses and chimneys and rising smoke and, finally, with a transcendent effort, of men who move dimly and already crumbling through the powdery air … the ash-gray men swarm up with leaden spades and stir up an impenetrable cloud …

Perkins preferred *The Great Gatsby* as a title, though acknowledging that at this early stage he had 'only the vaguest knowledge of the book'.[280] Free of financial anxiety and with a clearer mind, Fitzgerald made the momentous decision to discard 'a lot' of what he had written during the previous tumultuous summer, much of it 'so interrupted that it was ragged'.[281] He approached the story from a 'new angle'.

Out of an 18,000-word section of the discarded work, he crafted a short story, 'Absolution', which he sold to *American Mercury*. He had intended to use the story as the prologue of the novel providing a picture of the early life of his protagonist.[282] 'Absolution' is an autobiographical story of an eleven-year-old boy whose father failed to take advantage of the great business opportunities presented to him when he moved to the Midwest, and who ends up with a 'mystical worship' of James J. Hill.

> Hill was the apotheosis of that quality in which [he] him-
> self was deficient − the sense of things, the feel of things, the
> hint of rain in the wind on the cheek … His weary, sprightly,
> undersized body was growing old in Hill's gigantic shadow.
> For twenty years he had lived alone with Hill's name and God.

The boy's nervous mother receives little mention. His family is poorer than his neighbours and he is furiously ashamed when he has no money to drop in the collection box at Sunday mass. Bowing his head, he pretends not to see the box in case a young girl in the pew behind would 'suspect an acute family poverty'. The boy reimagines himself as the very English-sounding Blatchford Sarnemington to emancipate himself from his ineffectual parents. When he becomes this heroic and popular figure, 'a suave nobility flowed from him'.

The boy tells a lie in confession, as Fitzgerald had done at the same age, but the heart of the story is what he reveals about his attitude to his parents in the confessional box.[283] After confessing to being mean to an old lady who would not give back his baseball, the priest urges him to divulge more substantial sins:

'Go on, my child.'

'Of – of not believing I was the son of my parents.'

'What?' The interrogation was distinctly startled.

'Of not believing that I was the son of my parents.'

'Why not?'

'Oh, just pride,' answered the penitent airily.

'You mean you thought you were too good to be the son of your parents?'

'Yes, Father.'

Fitzgerald disguised his boyhood ethnic identity by naming the boy Rudolph Miller and hinting at a German or Swedish immigrant background; the celibate priest, the incongruously named Father Schwartz, is troubled by the 'rustle of Swede girls along the path by his window'. Fitzgerald seemed unable to bury fully his Irish identity, however. The boy's father arrived 'with the second wave of German and Irish stock to the Minnesota-Dakota country' and he named the girl at mass, Jeanne Brady.

'Absolution' had another purpose other than providing the origin story of his protagonist. The prologue was intended to set up themes of sexual freedom, extravagance and the search for illusion and wonder in the novel. During confession, in agony and with shame in his heart, the boy admits to the sins of 'dirty words and immodest thoughts and desires':

'Where were you when this happened?'

'Well, it was up in the loft of this barn and this girl and – a fella, they were saying things – saying immodest things, and I stayed.'

'You should have gone – you should have told the girl to go.'

He should have gone! He could not tell Father Schwartz how his pulse had bumped in his wrist, how a strange, romantic excitement had possessed him when those curious things had been said.

The bored, kind and lonely priest suppresses his own inner passions. As the story closes, he exhibits signs of a nervous breakdown, 'the beads of his rosary were crawling and squirming like snakes upon the green felt of his table top'. Longing to escape his monotonous Midwest life, he tells the boy that, 'when a whole lot of people get together in the best places things go glimmering all the time … The thing is to have a lot of people in the center of the world, wherever that happens to be.' To explain his meaning, he advises the boy to go to an amusement park:

'Go to one at night and stand a little way off from it in a dark place – under dark trees. You'll see a big wheel made of lights turning in the air, and a long slide shooting boats down into the water. A band playing somewhere, and a smell of peanuts – and everything will twinkle …'

The puzzled and frightened boy finds it strange and awful to hear a priest talk so. '"But don't get up close," he warned Rudolph, "because if you do you'll only feel the heat and the sweat and the life."'

But the boy wants to get up close. In a triumph of romanticism over the sexually repressive religion of the priest and his father, he feels his own inner convictions confirmed that: 'There was something ineffably gorgeous somewhere that had nothing to do with God.'

Fitzgerald abandoned the prologue to 'preserve a sense of mystery' around his protagonist.[284] As part of the new angle, he wanted him to be vague, blurry and enigmatic, and the prologue 'interfered with the neatness of the plan'.[285] In place of the prologue, he introduced a narrator, Nick Carraway, a Yale graduate from a well-to-do mercantile Midwest family. Restless after returning home from war, he moves east to learn the bond business and rents a small house in 'one of the strangest communities' in America on 'slender riotous' Long Island. He lives in West Egg village situated on a peninsula jutting into Long Island Sound, which is separated by a small bay from the more fashionable East Egg headland.

Carraway's little house stands next to an oversized imitation 'Hôtel de Ville' mansion owned by a man named Jay Gatsby, whom he sees driving a yellow Rolls Royce and wearing pink suits. Yet to be introduced to his neighbour, he is intrigued, 'young men didn't … drift coolly out of nowhere and buy a palace on Long Island Sound'.

The themes that had been set-up in 'Absolution' were not abandoned. Before he meets Gatsby in person, Carraway receives an invitation to a party at his house, which lights up like the 'world's fair' and where party-goers behave like they are at 'amusement parks':

> … men and girls came and went like moths among the whisperings and the champagne and the stars … The bar is in full swing, and floating rounds of cocktails permeate the garden outside … the orchestra is playing yellow cocktail music … By midnight the hilarity had increased. A celebrated tenor had sung in Italian, and a notorious contralto had sung in jazz, and between the numbers people were doing 'stunts' all over the garden … girls were putting their heads on men's shoulders in a puppyish, convivial way, girls were swooning backward playfully into men's arms …

Fitzgerald had input into the design of the cover jacket. Francis Cugat's iconic Art Deco image depicts a mysterious female face with the outline of eyes and red lips visible over a blue background, and at the bottom are the golden lights of night-time Coney Island.

Fitzgerald had an innate sense of the romantic and a heightened sense of wonder. He captured this in the autobiographical Rudolph Miller, who believes there is 'something ineffably gorgeous somewhere' and although he abandoned the prologue, he retained the sense of wonder in Jay Gatsby, who has 'something gorgeous about him; some heightened sensitivity to the promises of life ... an extraordinary gift for hope, a romantic readiness'.

EXILE

As winter turned to spring on Long Island, Fitzgerald became restless. The party season had come round again. Playwright and humourist George F. Kaufman threw a party at his home.[286] He wrote several musicals for the Marx Brothers and won a Pulitzer Prize in 1932 for the political satire musical, *Of Thee I Sing*. Fitzgerald believed he plagiarised the idea from *The Vegetable*.[287] He needed to concentrate on his work. He did not want a repeat of the constant drinking, the disorder and quarrels with Zelda and a house always full of people. He was 'bored and feeling bad' and tiring of his friends, and he made a spontaneous decision to move the family to France.

In early May the family steamed across the Atlantic on the S.S. *Minnewaska* carrying seventeen pieces of luggage, the Encyclopaedia Britannica and 100 feet of copper wire for the mosquitoes. His destination was not Paris, the expatriate home of many American writers, but the French Riviera, where the $7,000 in his bank account held significantly more purchasing power. During a brief stay in Paris, they hired an English nanny for $26 a month ('My God! We paid $90 in New York'), and lunched with John Peale Bishop, who had married into a wealthy family and after a period as managing editor at *Vanity Fair* had moved to France.

Fitzgerald eased into his new life in Hyères, a beautiful hillside town located between Marseille and Nice, looking forward to 'a gorgeous working summer'.[288] He painted the evening scene in a letter to Tom Boyd: 'Zelda and I are sitting in the café l'Universe writing letters … and the moon is an absolutely au fait Mediteraenean [*sic*] moon … we're both a little tight and very happily drunk.' Inspired by the setting and with renewed artistic confidence, he proclaimed to his protégé: 'I shall write a novel better than any novel ever written in America.'

But the early weeks on the Côte d'Azur proved more troublesome than expected. Struggling to find a villa, he stayed at the appropriately named Grimms Park Hotel where he found it difficult to work. 'So far I've only done one chapter [since the three written on Long Island],' he informed his agent Harold Ober in June, 'and I've been gone from America almost four weeks.'[289] A progress report to Perkins informed the editor that the novel was 'going fine', that it should be done in a month, but he was not sure as he was 'contemplating another 16,000 words'.[290]

Fitzgerald used the narrator Carraway to provide an abridged origin story for Gatsby; one with a twist because his neighbour in West Egg is, in fact, not Jay Gatsby, but Jimmy Gatz from the Midwest. His biography is sketchy, but he remains autobiographical, despite also being given German or Nordic ethnicity and possibly being

Lutheran, and being unclear if he is from Minnesota or North Dakota.[291] His helpless father considers James J. Hill to be a 'great man' who 'helped build up the country'. We learn nothing about his mother. And like the young Fitzgerald, and Amory Blaine and Rudolph Miller, Gatz's 'imagination had never really accepted them as his parents at all'. Fitzgerald uses Carraway to justify his rejection of his own parents and heritage: 'I understood what he meant … what better right does a man possess than to invent his own antecedents?'[292] Gatz escapes the Midwest and his parents – 'shiftless and unsuccessful' farming people – reinventing himself as the ethnically neutral Jay Gatsby.

Fitzgerald struggled with the transition of young Jimmy Gatz into adult Jay Gatsby. He introduced two contrived and exaggerated backstory incidents. At sixteen, Gatz makes his way along the shore of Lake Superior working as a fisherman and in any capacity that brought him food and a bed. An instinct toward 'future glory', echoing the 'marked for glory' of Amory Blaine, leads him to St Olaf's, a small Lutheran college in southern Minnesota founded by Norwegian pastors and farmers. He stays only two weeks 'dismayed at its ferocious indifference to the drums of his destiny, to destiny itself'. The scene is designed as a criticism of the limitations of the education he received at Newman and Princeton.

For the next stage of Gatz's evolution into Gatsby, he mined the experience of Robert Kerr, a friend he met in Great Neck. As a teenager, Kerr had befriended a

mysterious yachtsman – Dan Cody in the novel. 'I have
my hero occupy the same position you did,' Fitzgerald
wrote to him in June, 'and obtain it in the same way.'[293]
Returning to Lake Superior, Gatz in a torn green jersey
and a pair of canvas pants spies Cody's yacht anchored at
a dangerous location on the lake. He borrows a rowboat,
becomes Jay Gatsby and informs Cody that a wind might
catch him and break him up. Cody finds him 'quick,
and extravagantly ambitious'. The reinvented Gatsby
becomes a loyal and trustworthy associate of the self-
made copper-mining millionaire pioneer. They sail to the
West Indies, the Barbary Coast and 'three times around
the continent' over five years. On Cody's unexpected
death, Gatz is cheated out of a $25,000 inheritance leav-
ing him broke.

Fitzgerald explains the *nouveau riche* aspirations of the
reinvented Gatsby using philosophical references and
religious symbolism:

> The truth was that Jay Gatsby of West Egg, Long Island,
> sprang from his Platonic conception [the perfect or ideal
> form] of himself. He was a son of God – a phrase which, if it
> means anything, means just that – and he must be about His
> Father's business, the service of a vast, vulgar, and meretri-
> cious beauty. So he invented just the sort of Jay Gatsby that a
> seventeen-year-old boy would be likely to invent, and to this
> conception he was faithful to the end.

After stitching together this unlikely backstory, Fitzgerald skips five years without explanation until Gatsby
receives a commission as a lieutenant, aligning the story
again with his own life.

Incorruptible Dream

Hyerés proved too hot, the mosquitoes terrorist-like, locals continually took advantage and goat meat was ubiquitous on the hotel menu. Unable to rent a clean villa, with Zelda he explored alternative locations along the coast and they entertained themselves in the finest establishments. The Hotel de Paris in Monte Carlo was like 'a palace in a detective story', and when dining on the elegant terrace of the Hotel Ruhl in Nice 'stars fell in our plates'.[294] They eventually found the charming Villa Marie in St Raphael a short distance up the coast from Hyerés.

The move to the Villa Marie proved a good one. 'My book is wonderful, so is the air and the sea,' he wrote to Edmund Wilson. 'I have got my health back – I no longer cough and itch and roll from one side of the bed to the other all night and have a hollow ache in my stomach after two cups of black coffee.'[295] On 23 June, he wrote to Boyd that the novel was 'almost done'.[296]

Gatsby, on receiving his commission as a lieutenant, is posted to Camp Taylor near Louisville and sets his sights on Daisy Fay. Like Zelda, she is the most popular girl; excited officers demand the privilege of monopolising her time. Gatsby likes that many men had already loved her: 'it increased her value in his eyes'. Daisy has elements of Ginevra; she is the first 'nice' girl he has ever known. In his previous encounters with the wealthy, there had been 'indiscernible barbed wire' between them. Her house has an air of mystery and of romance, he appreciates how wealth preserves youth and mystery, and he watches Daisy 'safe and proud above the hot struggles of the poor'.

Gatsby understands that dating a beautiful rich girl is an accident of fate. He might have a glorious future, but at present he was 'a penniless young man without a past, and at any moment the invisible cloak of his uniform might slip from his shoulders'.

> He took what he could get, ravenously and unscrupulously – eventually he took Daisy one still October night, took her because he had no real right to touch her hand.
>
> … he had deliberately given Daisy a sense of security; he let her believe that he was a person from much the same stratum as herself – that he was fully able to take care of her. As a matter of fact he had no such facilities – he had no comfortable family standing behind him and he was liable at the whim of an impersonal government to be blown anywhere about the world.

Daisy is refused permission by her mother to go to New York to say goodbye to Gatsby as he goes to war. Heartbroken, she waits for his return and stops meeting other officers. But soon, she is 'gay again, gay as ever'. When the war ends, Gatsby tries frantically to get home, but is prevented by 'some complication or misunderstanding'. Fitzgerald likes to avoid long explanations. And like Fitzgerald reading Zelda's letters in New York, Gatsby sees 'nervous despair' in her correspondence; she doesn't see why he can't come back to her.

Daisy returns to her world of 'cheerful snobbery and orchestras which set the rhythm of the year'. She wants her life now; there is a rumour of an engagement. Then, another man appears in her life. He is Tom Buchanan from Chicago with a home at Lake Forest, 'enormously wealthy', Ivy League educated, a polo-player. He is William Mitchell on the outside, but is caricatured as a symbol of the careless elite. Supercilious and fractious, he has a body capable of enormous leverage, 'a cruel body'. Tom comes to Louisville to marry Daisy and gives her a pearl necklace valued at $350,000.

Daisy writes to Gatsby with a 'certain struggle and a certain relief'. Like Zelda, she is prepared to close out the relationship on the basis of common sense. When a letter arrives from him half an hour before the bridal dinner, Daisy proceeds to get 'drunk as a monkey' and desperately cries out to her bridesmaid that she has changed her mind. Next day, she marries Tom Buchanan 'without so much as a shiver'. They spend a year in France 'for no particular reason' and then drift 'to wherever people played polo and were rich together', until Tom buys a Georgian Colonial mansion on the elite East Egg peninsula facing the bay. Here they reunite with Carraway, the narrator, who was in Yale with Tom and is a second cousin once removed to Daisy.

Gatsby, disconsolate, returns from war when the newly-weds are on honeymoon. He makes a 'miserable but irresistible journey' to Louisville on the last of his army pay. He returns penniless to New York on the steaming hot day-coach and from there builds up a vast illusion and self-deception that Daisy's marriage to Tom is a 'terrible mistake' and in her heart she never loved anyone but him; it was impossible that she could love anyone else; she married Tom because he was poor and she was tired of waiting; he would win her back. His romantic quest is an 'incorruptible dream'.

DRIVE TO DESTRUCTION

In the new age of mass communication, consumption and mobility, the automobile became a plaything and status symbol. An image of a boyhood rival, Reuben Warner, sitting aloof at the wheel of his Stutz Bearcat, was imprinted in Fitzgerald's memory.[297]

Once when Max Perkins and his wife came to Long Island, an inebriated Fitzgerald drove them straight into a lake in his second-hand Rolls-Royce.

On the French Riviera, Fitzgerald had to settle for a little Renault car, but he filled his novel with automotive symbols and driving motifs. Wild car rides, accidents and car swaps drive the Gatsby narrative, and the social status, personality and value system of each character is revealed by what and how they drive.

The *nouveau riche* Gatsby living in up-and-coming West Egg owns a 'swollen … monstrous' yellow Rolls Royce. The *old money* Tom drives an elegant blue coupé. Shortly after marrying Daisy, he drives into a wagon, rips a front wheel off his car and a hotel chambermaid with whom he is having an affair has her arm broken; women in Tom's life end up with emotional and physical scars. Daisy, innocent on the surface, had a 'little white roadster' as a teenager in segregated Louisville.

Tom's mistress, the sensuous Myrtle, has 'a vitality about her as if the nerves of her body were continually smouldering' and is married to the ghostlike George Wilson, the proprietor of an unprosperous motor garage in the valley of the ashes. Wilson is spiritless and anaemic like the only car visible inside his garage, 'a dust-covered wreck of a Ford which crouched in a dim corner'. Tom, who had promised to sell one of his cars to Wilson, considers him 'so dumb he doesn't know he's alive'. Myrtle believes her husband tricked her into marriage. They had lived over the garage in the valley of ashes for eleven years when she saw Tom on the train: 'All I kept thinking about, over and over, was "You can't live forever, you can't live forever."' She believes he is going to marry her, a ticket out of the ashes, but to him she is another possession, another plaything. At a small party in an apartment he keeps in the city, Carraway witnesses Tom break her nose with his open hand when she mentions Daisy's name.

Carraway, a trainee bond salesman, drives an 'old Dodge'. His girlfriend Jordan Baker is named for two automobile brands; the manufacturer Jordan Motor and the luxury fabric supplier Baker Motor. Contemptuous, distant and insolent, the model of her car is not revealed. Her character is partly modelled on Edith Cummings, a friend of Ginevra King and an elite golfer, but Jordan is an 'incurably dishonest' golf cheat. Carraway's attraction is part superficial, wanting to be seen out with a golf champion, and part curiosity and fascination. Maybe this is understandable for a young man from the Midwest experiencing city high life for the first time.

Jordan is part of the elite 'rotten crowd'. Driving home from a party with Caraway in her car, she passes much too close to some workmen. Nick protests that she is a 'rotten driver' and that she ought to be more careful or not drive at all:

'I am careful.'

'No, you're not.'

'Well, other people are,' she said lightly.

'What's that got to do with it?'

'They'll keep out of my way,' she insisted.

Gatsby enters the story in person almost a third of the way into the novel; part of the plan to keep him vague and mysterious, though Carraway sees him earlier from his small garden on a summer's evening. In an exercise of prose and descriptive skill, Fitzgerald introduces an aspirational and yearning tone to the novel:

The wind had blown off, leaving a loud bright night with wings beating in the trees and a persistent organ sound as the full bellows of the earth blew the frogs full of life. The silhouette of a moving cat wavered across the moonlight and turning my head to watch it I saw that I was not alone – fifty feet away a figure had emerged from the shadow of my neighbor's mansion and was standing with his hands in his pockets regarding the silver pepper of the stars ... Mr. Gatsby himself, come out to determine what share was his of our local heavens.

... he stretched out his arms toward the dark water in a curious way, and, far as I was from him, I could have sworn he was trembling. Involuntarily I glanced seaward – and distinguished nothing except a single green light, minute and far away, that might have been the end of a dock. When I looked once more for Gatsby he had vanished, and I was alone again in the unquiet darkness.

The iconic green light was indeed at the end of a dock. Gatsby had bought his house so that Daisy would be just across the bay. He half expected her to wander into one of his parties. He began asking people casually if they knew her.

Carraway first hears wild speculation about his neighbour at the party in Tom's city apartment:

'Well, they say he's a nephew or a cousin of Kaiser Wilhelm's. That's where all his money comes from.'
'I'm scared of him. I'd hate to have him get anything on me.'

Even before Tom brutally hits Myrtle, Carraway had wanted to leave, but each time he makes to go he becomes entangled in a strident argument. He looks out the window and sees himself, like Fitzgerald, as being inside and outside of society:

> Yet high over the city our line of yellow windows must have contributed their share of human secrecy to the casual watcher in the darkening streets, and I was him too, looking up and wondering. I was within and without, simultaneously enchanted and repelled by the inexhaustible variety of life.

He hears more 'romantic speculation' and 'babbled slander' about Gatsby amid floating rounds of cocktails and profusions of champagne after receiving an invitation to a party at his neighbour's house. The opinions are proffered by guests who, like Carraway, have never met the host in person, in an atmosphere 'alive with chatter and laughter and casual innuendo and introductions forgotten on the spot':

> 'Somebody told me they thought he killed a man once.'
> 'It's more that he was a German spy during the war' …
> 'I heard that from a man who knew all about him, grew up with him in Germany,' …
> 'it couldn't be that, because he was in the American army during the war.'
> 'You look at him sometimes when he thinks nobody's looking at him. I'll *bet* [FSF italics] he killed a man.'

'He's a bootlegger … One time he killed a man who had
found out that he was nephew to von Hindenburg and second
cousin to the devil.'

Three of the comments imply Gatsby 'killed a man',
the same phrase used each time, but each time in a way
that raises doubts; it is third-hand speculation, a guess
worth a bet and linked to an outlandish claim that he is
the second cousin to the devil.

Carraway meets Gatsby for the first time at the party
unaware that he is talking to him: '"I thought you knew,
old sport. I'm afraid I'm not a very good host."'

The familiar old sport expression 'held no more famil-
iarity than the hand which reassuringly brushed my
shoulder', and before him Carraway saw, 'an elegant
young rough-neck, a year or two over thirty, whose elaborate formality of speech just missed being absurd'.
During the course of the evening, Gatsby is interrupted
twice by a butler informing him of important calls from
Chicago and Philadelphia, hinting at some form of illegal
activity. Leaving to return home, Carraway sees a new
coupé, owned by a drunk party-goer, in a ditch beside
the road, right side up, but 'violently shorn of one wheel'.

Shortly after, Gatsby drives him in the Rolls Royce into
the city for lunch. He arrives outside the small house
'balancing himself on the dashboard of his car with that
resourcefulness of movement that is so peculiarly American'. He had found out that Carraway knew Daisy and
wants him to invite her to tea and let him come over for

a surprise reunion. Gatsby also wants to account for the 'bizarre accusations' made against him. Keen that Carraway does not get a wrong idea, he tells him the 'God's truth' about his life. As they drive through West Egg Village on their way to the city, he listens to an elaborate fabricated origin tale that has no resemblance to the real life of Jimmy Gatz: '"I am the son of some wealthy people in the middle-west – all dead now. I was brought up in America but educated at Oxford because all my ancestors have been educated there for many years. It is a family tradition."'

Carraway senses that he might be lying and wonders if 'there wasn't something a little sinister about him after all'. Hearing that he is from San Francisco, which he calls the Midwest, and that after his family all died he came into a good deal of money, Carraway suspects that Gatsby is pulling his leg, but a glance and his solemn tone convinces him otherwise. But he struggles to restrain 'incredulous laughter' when Gatsby tells him that he 'lived like a young rajah in all the capitals of Europe – Paris, Venice, Rome – collecting jewels, chiefly rubies, hunting big game, painting a little, things for myself only, and trying to forget something very sad that had happened to me long ago'. Fascination overtakes incredulity when Gatsby turns himself into such a heroic war hero that every Allied government gave him a decoration, 'even Montenegro, little Montenegro down on the Adriatic Sea!'

They motor through the valley of the ashes and Carraway sees Myrtle Wilson 'straining at the garage pump with panting vitality'. Gatsby manages to establish the veracity of his tale by showing him the medal presented by the Montenegrin government: 'To my astonishment, the thing had an authentic look.' He produces a photograph of himself with half a dozen young men in blazers taken in Trinity Quad at Oxford University. Carraway believes him, even when a motor cycle policeman lets them off a speeding charge because Gatsby had done the commissioner a favour once.

They drive over the Queensboro bridge. Irish-Americans had objected to the royal name preferring an American one like 'Montauk'.[298] Fitzgerald again exercised his sparkling prose and symbolism, mainly automotive, to capture the magic of New York City and the changing face of American society, and to make us believe that anything is possible:

The city seen from the Queensboro Bridge is always the city seen for the first time, in its first wild promise of all the mystery and the beauty in the world.

A dead man passed us in a hearse heaped with blooms, followed by two carriages with drawn blinds and by more cheerful carriages for friends. The friends looked out at us with the tragic eyes and short upper lips of south-eastern Europe, and I was glad that the sight of Gatsby's splendid car was included in their somber holiday.

As we crossed Blackwell's Island a limousine passed us, driven by a white chauffeur, in which sat three modish Negroes, two bucks and a girl. I laughed aloud as the yolks of their eyeballs rolled toward us in haughty rivalry.

'Anything can happen now that we've slid over this bridge,' I thought; 'anything at all...'

Even Gatsby could happen, without any particular wonder.

MOBSTERS

Settling comfortably into the Villa Maria and life on the Côte d'Azur, the Fitzgeralds hosted their first dinner party in June and sat up all night in the warm air. In 'How to Live on Practically Nothing a Year', a piece he wrote to shore up his dwindling capital, Fitzgerald poked fun at the 'two reformed spendthrifts' escaping from the 'wild extremes among which we had dwelt for five hectic years'.[299] With no intention of integrating with the locals or learning the language, he self-mockingly wrote: '"Je suis a stranger here," I said in flawless French. "Je veux aller to le best hotel dans le town."'

He spent his days writing, while Zelda with Scottie and the governess in tow went swimming and sunbathing on a sandy beach. Though weary of sharp local tradesmen and worried by the high cost of living on the Riviera, he wrote to Boyd that 'everything's idyllic'. For the first time in three years he was perfectly happy.[300] They ventured up and down the coast in the little Renault, taking in Nice and Monaco, which Somerset Maugham described as 'a sunny place for shady people'.

Fitzgerald had previous experience with shady people. One year earlier, on 20 July 1923, a mid-ranking racketeer in New York named Max Gerlach bought a newspaper, clipped a picture and added a note on top: 'En route from the coast – Here for a few days on business – How are you and the family *old Sport*?.' The clipping was a portrait of the Fitzgerald family reclining on the lawn of their home on Long Island. Gerlach was likely on bootlegging business at the coast. Fitzgerald posted the picture in his scrapbook.

Zelda suggested in a later interview that Gatsby was modelled on 'a neighbor named von Guerlach or something who was said to be General Pershing's nephew and was in trouble over bootlegging'.[301] In 1951, Gerlach identified himself as the inspiration for the protagonist. By then, he was blind after an attempted suicide by shooting.

Born in 1885 in Germany, Gerlach emigrated with his mother and stepfather at age nine. His birth father was a secretary to Frederick III in the Ministry of the Royal House of Hohenzollern. According to Horst H. Kruse, who unearthed much of the background on the mysterious and shady hoodlum, he used his stepfather's last name, Stork, for nearly two decades and presented various contradictory versions of his life story.[302]

As a teenager in Yonkers, he accidently shot dead his eleven-month-old brother and became involved in petty crime.[303] Gerlach trained as an automobile mechanic and worked as a marine gas engineer. A Spanish speaker, he spent time in Cuba racing cars and opening a garage. During the war, according to another Gerlach scholar Alan Sargeant, he made frequent unexplained trips between Berlin and Cuba, either 'part of some illegal, mobster enterprise or some clandestine mission for the

US military'.[304] After the war he worked for automobile dealers and also sold high-end vehicles as a broker, possibly selling a second-hand Marmon sports coupé to Fitzgerald.[305] His ready access to illicit alcohol might have cemented their relationship.

Fitzgerald used Gerlach as a model for Gatsby's surface mannerisms, including the 'old sport' expression, and for his fabricated backstory. A ready myth-maker, Gerlach claimed to have been educated at an English university, spoke with an 'Oxford accent' and said that he had served as a major during the war though he had only ever been a first lieutenant.[306] He inspired much of the 'romantic speculation' and 'babbled slander' about Gatsby. Though growing up in Germany, he had joined the American Army and he was suspected of being a German spy. Speculation that Gatsby was a nephew to von Hindenburg and a cousin of Kaiser Wilhelm bares some similarity to Gerlach who sometimes used the nobility predicate 'von' and claimed that he was the son of a German baron.[307]

Gatsby's extravagant *nouveau riche* exterior – the imitation French villa, the garish Rolls Royce, the pink suits and the imported shirts – was inspired by another gangster. During the summer of 1923 Zelda had written to friends in St Paul: 'I have unearthed some of the choicest bootleggers (including Fleischman).'[308] Around the same time, Edmund Wilson was writing *The Crime in the Whistler Room* whose protagonist, a bootlegger named Max Fleischman, bragged about 'how much his tapestries were worth and how much his bathroom was worth and how he never wore a shirt twice'. Fitzgerald annotated a copy of the play next to a description of Fleischman: 'I had told Bunny my plan for Gatsby.'[309]

In his own novel, Daisy accepts Carraway's invitation to tea, Gatsby drops by and a magical reunion takes place after some initial embarrassment on both sides. Fitzgerald does not give a reason why Daisy so quickly turns her back on her marriage, other than that she is aware of Tom's infidelity, and according to Jordan Baker: 'Daisy ought to have something in her life.' Gatsby, like Myrtle for Tom, is her plaything.

He shows off his house to her. As they wander through Marie Antoinette music rooms, restoration salons and period bedrooms, he is 'consumed with wonder at her presence'. When they reach his bedroom, Daisy takes a brush with delight and smooths her hair. The image is almost too much for him to absorb after the intensity of his five-year quest. He takes out a pile of shirts and begins throwing them, one by one, 'shirts of sheer linen and thick silk and fine flannel which lost their folds as they fell and covered the table in many-colored disarray.' '"They're such beautiful shirts," she sobbed, her voice muffled in the thick folds. "It makes me sad because I've never seen such – such beautiful shirts before."'

The sentiment matches Fitzgerald's later recollection of life in New York in 1920 after the success of *This Side of Paradise*: 'I remember riding in a taxi one afternoon between very tall buildings under a mauve and rosy sky;

I began to bawl because I had everything I wanted and knew I would never be so happy again.'[310]

Arnold Rothstein, a top crime boss, directly inspired another important character in the novel, Meyer Wolfsheim, a Jewish mobster. Newspapers carefully referred to Rothstein as the 'reputed gambler and real estate and insurance man', while his crime associates knew him as 'The Brain'. He controlled wealthy bankers and influential politicians, and his criminal organisation included Charles 'Lucky' Luciano and Meyer Lansky. He was godfather to the godfathers. Rothstein was suspected of fixing the 1919 Baseball World Series. In the final game, a slugfest at Comisky Park, the Cincinnati Reds beat the Chicago White Sox 5–3. Rumours were rife, however, that the White Sox had thrown the series. Hugh Fullerton in the New York *Evening Post* would run a story, 'Is Big League Baseball Being Run for Gamblers, with Players in the Deal?' Eight White Sox players were banned from the game for life, including the great 'Shoeless Joe' Jackson whose innocence is still debated today.

More than anyone Rothstein saw in advance the vast sums of money to be made in bootlegging. He knew that high-end liqueur would be the 'chic thing to have'.[311] Thanks to his illegal and thuggish entrepreneurship, New York and Long Island continued to party through prohibition. He owned a building at 51 West 58th Street where Gerlach operated a speakeasy.[312]

Shortly after moving to Long Island, Fitzgerald attended an extravagant party thrown by Herbert Swope, the well-known editor of the *New York World* and a good friend of Ring Lardner who had been involved in uncovering the baseball scandal. Ironically, Swope was also an intimate friend of Arnold Rothstein.[313]

Fitzgerald wrote to a friend that for his novel he had 'selected the stuff to fit a given planned mood or "haunt-edness" or whatever you might call it … always starting from the small focal point that impressed me − my own meeting with Arnold Rothstein for instance'.[314] However, he turned Rothstein, as Meyer Wolfsheim, into a crude caricature of a Jewish gangster baring no physical likeness to his well-groomed model. At lunch in the city with Gatsby, Carraway is introduced to Wolfsheim in a dimly-lit 42nd Street speakeasy cellar: 'A small, flat-nosed Jew raised his large head and regarded me with two fine growths of hair which luxuriated in either nostril. After a moment I discovered his tiny eyes in the half darkness.'

He learns from Wolfsheim that he first met Gatsby when he was just out of the army and had to keep on wearing his uniform because he couldn't buy regular clothes. Wolfsheim saw a man 'of fine breeding … the kind of man you'd like to take home and introduce to your mother and sister'. He had 'made him … raised him up out of nothing, right out of the gutter'.

THE BIG CRISIS

Fitzgerald wrote to Max Perkins from the Villa Marie on 10 July 1924: 'I'm not going to mention my novel to you again until it is on your desk. All goes well ... Do write me a nice long letter.'[315] Calm lasted three days. His married life was about to be turned upside down. Fitzgerald's ledger entry for the month reads: 'The Big crisis – 13th of July.'

Fitzgerald and Zelda entered marriage with contrasting personalities and a shared self-destructive disposition. His Princeton friends in New York after the war, eager to meet Zelda, called on the newly-weds. Alexander McKaig noted in his diary: 'I do not think marriage can succeed. Both drinking heavily. Think they will be divorced in 3 years.'[316] He visited them again during a boisterous sojourn in Westport, Connecticut, in the summer of 1920: 'Terrible party. Fitz & Zelda fighting like mad – say themselves marriage can't succeed.'

Living a life of public notoriety, without care of what the world thought, or of the future, Fitzgerald later wrote of their early life in New York: 'we scarcely knew any more who we were and we hadn't a notion what we were. A dive into a civic fountain, a casual brush with the law, was enough to get us into the gossip columns, and we were quoted on a variety of subjects we knew nothing about.' Behind their public front lay loneliness and disconnection. Neither could fit in with general society. He remembered 'a lonesome Christmas when we had not one friend in the city, nor one house we could go to'.[317]

At least he had his writing; Zelda was directionless. He had college friends in New York. She was a newly arrived southern girl, with no interest in mingling with the young married set and ill-suited to a life of domesticity, and she lacked an outlet for her unfulfilled creative talent. When McKaig met them again in October he noted: 'Usual problem there. What shall Zelda do? … If she's there Fitz can't work – she bothers him – if she's not there he can't work – worried of what she might do.' He suggested that Zelda go into the movies. Another evening spent with the Fitzgeralds did not auger well: 'Fitz has been on wagon 8 days – talks as if it were a century. Zelda increasingly restless … what is she to do? Fitz has his writing of course – God knows where the two of them are going to end up.'

Four years later in the South of France, Zelda's lack of fulfilment remained an issue. He spent long hours working on the novel. With a villa full of servants and a nanny to mind Scottie, she was bored, restless and maybe exhibiting early signs of a later breakdown. Fitzgerald used her emotional state in his characterisation of Daisy:

I woke up out of the ether with an utterly abandoned feeling, and asked the nurse right away if it was a boy or a girl. She told me it was a girl, and so I turned my head away and wept.

'All right,' I said, 'I'm glad it's a girl. And I hope she'll be a fool
– that's the best thing a girl can be in this world, a beautiful
little fool ...

'What'll we do with ourselves this afternoon,' cried Daisy, 'and
the day after that, and the next thirty years?'

An encounter with three young French aviators based
in nearby Fréjus, a port town with a Roman amphithe-
atre and aqueduct, brought excitement into Zelda's life.
Young, sun-drenched, bronzed and dazzling in their
starched white shirts, Edouard Jozan, René Silvé and
Bobbé Croirier became beach friends for her during the
day. She must have had a sense of *déjà vu*; a reincarnation
of happy dreamy days entertaining officers in Montgomery. They even buzzed their planes low over the Villa
Marie. Fitzgerald joined them through warm mediterra-
nean evenings dancing and drinking in cafes, or at dinner
parties at the Villa Marie.

Zelda was drawn to Jozan, a year older, handsome,
muscular and a natural leader of men. While Fitzgerald was self-absorbed in pursuit of literary greatness and
admiration, with French ease Jozan lavished attention on
her; alone and without friends she craved it. He was 'full
of the sun'; her husband was a 'moon person'.[318]

Fitzgerald had an uncanny faculty for prophesy. Five
years earlier, when finishing *This Side of Paradise* in St
Paul, he had written to Edmund Wilson, who was putting
together a collection of stories about the war: 'I have just
the story for your book. It's not written yet. An Ameri-

can girl falls in love with an officer Francais at a southern camp.'[319]

Maybe it was just a summer flirtation. Jozan later insisted that any infidelity was purely imaginary: 'they both had a need of drama, they made it up and perhaps they were the victims of their own unsettled and a little unhealthy imagination'.[320] He may have been right, as both exaggerated the affair in later dramatic accounts and in its retelling to friends. Jozan was posted to Indochina and never saw them again, becoming a pioneer of carrier-based aviation and retiring with the rank of admiral.

The affair scarred Fitzgerald, heightening his insecurity and playing on his sensitive ego. Six years after, he wrote to Zelda who was in a psychiatric clinic at the time: 'I had been unhappy for a long time then − When my play failed a year and a half before, when I worked so hard for a year … with no one believing in me and no one to see except you and before the end your heart betraying me.'[321] Zelda accepted responsibility: 'We were alone, and gave big parties for the French aviators. Then there was Josen and you were justifiably angry.'[322]

The crisis happened at a bad time. Fitzgerald had learned nothing from his overspending days. He contacted his literary agent Harold Ober seeking an advance of $500 on a story. Kidding himself that they were 'living very cheaply', he appealed to him: 'After last winter I hate to ask you again and I am not absolutely strapped but being abroad I get nervous when the account gets low at the bank.' Encouragingly, though optimistically, he was certain that 'the novel is almost done'.[323]

Three weeks later, on 6 August, he went on the wagon and managed 'Good work on novel'.[324] By the end of the month, he and Zelda were 'close together'. Visiting and new friends helped the healing process. Writer, critic and broadcaster Gilbert Seldes, and his wife Amanda, came south after their marriage in Paris. Seldes had positively reviewed *Ulysses* two years earlier, though the book would remain banned in America for another decade. They met the writer Dos Passos and Gerald and Sara Murphy, who became close though sometimes exasperated friends of the Fitzgeralds; they tolerated his drunken antics and sophomoric humour, more concerned than reproachful. He admired their use of wealth as patrons of the arts. Gerald's Irishness provided a common bond. As Edmund Wilson was his intellectual conscience, he looked to Murphy 'to dictate my relations with other people when these relations were successful: how to do, what to say. How to make people at least momentarily happy ... This always confused me and made me want to go out and get drunk.'[325]

He informed Perkins on 27 August that the 'novel will be done next week'.[326] He planned to take a week off, and then with Zelda do 'a careful revision'. His excitement was palpable, 'I think my novel is about the best American novel ever written.' He cautioned Perkins that it was 'rough stuff in places' and he hoped he wouldn't shy at it. He explained to him that he had been unhappy but his work had not suffered, and, 'I am grown at last.' When summer turned to autumn, Scott and Zelda spent their evenings on the beach and their trouble was clearing away.[327] His true feelings came out years later in his notebooks: 'That September 1924, I knew something had happened that could never be repaired.'[328] His emotional state added depth to his novel.

Gatsby feels betrayed by Daisy for abandoning him five years earlier and believes that she owes him.

> He seemed to feel that Daisy should make some sort of atonement that would give her love the value that it had before … he wanted this to have an element of fate about it, of inevitability – the resumption of an uninterrupted dance. And first Daisy must purify herself by a renunciation of the years between.
>
> '… I used to think wonderful things were going to happen to me, before I met her. And I knew it was a great mistake for a man like me to fall in love – and then one night I let myself go, and it was too late –.'[329]

Fitzgerald deleted this section. Daisy no longer needed to make atonement or purify herself. However, Carraway had perceived a faint doubt in Gatsby as to the quality of his happiness having recovered her. He wondered if, after five years, there had been moments when Daisy tumbled short of his dreams, 'not through her own fault but because of the colossal vitality of his illusion'. Gatsby's doubts disappear when Daisy whispers something low in his ear and he is filled with a rush of emotion:

> 'Her voice is full of money,' he said suddenly [to Carraway later]
> That was it. I'd never understood before. It was full of money – that was the inexhaustible charm that rose and fell in it, the jingle of it, the cymbals' song of it… High in a white palace the king's daughter, the golden girl …

Like Fitzgerald's love for Ginevra, the *'king's* daughter', Gatsby found Daisy's status and wealth irresistible.

POLITE INDIFFERENCE

When Fitzgerald delineated the social stratification of St Paul of his youth, at the bottom were certain rich newcomers, 'mysterious, out of a cloudy past, possibly unsound'.[330] To Tom Buchanan and the old money residents of East Egg across the bay, the new monied, immigrant-class Gatsby was a threat to their established Anglo-Saxon social order. He was worthy only of their careless disregard and polite disdain, the same Fitzgerald experienced at Lake Forest and in his dream. When East Egg deigns to attend his parties, it is with 'contemptuous interest'. At one party, Carraway is invited by Jordan to join her friends at a table on the other side of the garden, where the elite group 'preserved a dignified homogeneity, and assumed to itself the function of representing the staid nobility of the countryside – East Egg condescending to West Egg, and carefully on guard against its spectroscopic gayety'.

One Sunday afternoon after arranging the reconciliation between Gatsby and Daisy, Carraway goes over to his neighbour's house when a party of three on horseback call in for a drink; a man named Sloane, a 'pretty woman' who had been there previously, and to his shock, Tom Buchanan. This was not a social call, they just needed a drink. Gatsby is affected by Tom's presence and uneasy about the social class of his callers. This was not Gatsby's first encounter with Tom. Carraway had made a brief introduction when they accidently bumped into each other at the speakeasy on 42nd street. Gatsby reminds Tom that they had met, but he does not initially remember. Daringly, he says that he knows his wife, but Tom dismisses the comment with a 'That so?', hardly comprehending how it could even be possible.

Sloane lounges back haughtily in his chair, barely engaging with his host's polite conversation and refusing successive offers of a cigarette, a cigar and a drink. He wants to start for home. The woman says nothing, until two highballs are consumed and she enthusiastically invites Gatsby and Carraway to supper. The latter politely declines the invitation. Gatsby doesn't see that Sloane does not want them along; he says that he will follow in his car and excuses himself for a moment, leaving the group on the porch:

'My God, I believe the man's coming,' said Tom. 'Doesn't he know she doesn't want him?'

'She says she does want him.'

'She has a big dinner party and he won't know a soul there.' He frowned. 'I wonder where in the devil he met Daisy. By God, I may be old-fashioned in my ideas, but women run around too much these days to suit me. They meet all kinds of crazy fish.'

Tom, Sloane and the woman walk down the steps, mount their horses and trot quickly down the drive, disappearing just as Gatsby with hat and light overcoat in hand comes out of the front door.

Uneasy about Daisy running around alone, Tom comes to Gatsby's next party with her. He is arrogantly unimpressed, but eyes up a 'common but pretty' girl. Daisy sardonically offers him her little gold pencil to take down any addresses. Despite an attempt at gaiety, she, too, is offended by the scenes around her:

> She was appalled by West Egg, this unprecedented 'place' that Broadway had begotten upon a Long Island fishing village – appalled by its raw vigor that chafed under the old euphemisms and by the too obtrusive fate that herded its inhabitants along a short cut from nothing to nothing. She saw something awful in the very simplicity she failed to understand.

Unimpressed by the zoo-like behaviour, Tom expresses his suspicions as to the source of Gatsby's wealth to Carraway:

> 'Who is this Gatsby anyhow?' demanded Tom suddenly.
> 'Some big bootlegger?'
> 'Where'd you hear that?' I inquired.

'I didn't hear it. I imagined it. A lot of these newly rich people are just big bootleggers, you know.'

'Not Gatsby,' I said shortly.

He was silent for a moment. The pebbles of the drive crunched under his feet.

'Well, he certainly must have strained himself to get this menagerie together.' ...

'I'd like to know who he is and what he does,' insisted Tom. 'And I think I'll make a point of finding out.'

REPEAT THE PAST

Before Fitzgerald commenced writing the novel, he explained his artistic goal to Perkins, 'I want to write something new – something extraordinary and beautiful and simple and intricately patterned.'[331] In a letter to an admirer, he outlined his approach, 'I am so anxious for people to see my new novel which is a new thinking out of the idea of illusion … The business of creating illusion is much more to my taste and my talent.'[332]

His recent bitter life experience added a layer of disillusion on top of the illusion and wonder he had had beginning the novel; financial pressure, the failure of his play, more financial pressure, forced to write stories, Zelda's affair and his own tendency towards dissipation. He gloomily wrote to Ludlow Fowler, a Newman and Princeton classmate, and his best man: 'I remember our last conversation and it makes me sad. I feel old too, this summer – I have ever since the failure of my play a year ago. Thats [sic] the whole burden of this novel – the loss of those illusions that give such color to the world so that you don't care whether things are true or false as long as they partake of the magical glory.'[333]

He yearned for his younger days that were full of wonder and infinite opportunity. 'I don't want to repeat my innocence,' he wrote in *This Side of Paradise*. 'I want the pleasure of losing it again.' He sent a letter to Harold Ober: 'I'm twenty eight [*sic*]. I was twenty-two when I came to New York and found that you'd sold *Head and Shoulders* to the *Post*. I'd like to get a thrill like that again but I suppose it's only once in a lifetime.'[334] 'Head and Shoulders' was the first story he sold to the *Saturday Evening Post*. The young protagonist, Horace Tarbox, an intellectual prodigy at Princeton destined for a successful academic career, regrets falling for a spirited dancer.

Fitzgerald wanted to return to that point in his life when it was most open to possibility. Alcohol would soon become his time travel machine: 'The drink made past happy things contemporary with the present, as if they were still going on, contemporary even with the future as if they were about to happen again.' During the summer of 1924, it was his novel that offered the possibility of time travel.

Carraway stays late at the party, well after Tom and Daisy go home. Gatsby explains that he wants Daisy to tell Tom that she *never* loved him. By doing so, the past would be 'obliterated'. After she was free, they would go back to Louisville and be married from her house, 'just as if it were five years ago'. Carraway advises a more practical approach:

> 'I wouldn't ask too much of her,' he ventured. 'You can't repeat the past.'

'Can't repeat the past?' He cried incredulously. 'Why of course you can!' … 'I'm going to fix everything just the way it was before,' he said, nodding determinedly. 'She'll see.'

Gatsby wanted 'to recover something, some idea of himself perhaps, that had gone into loving Daisy. His life had been confused and disordered since, but if he could once return to a certain starting place and go over it all slowly, he could find out what that thing was.'

In a gratuitous exercise of prose and tone virtuosity, Fitzgerald offers a surreal explanation of 'that thing' that Gatsby – and he – had lost. Gatsby and Daisy were walking down a street on an autumn night in Louisville before he went to war. They stopped and turned toward each other:

Out of the corner of his eye Gatsby saw that the blocks of the sidewalk really formed a ladder and mounted to a secret place above the trees – he could climb to it, if he climbed alone, and once there he could suck on the pap of life, gulp down the incomparable milk of wonder.

His heart beat faster and faster as Daisy's white face came up to his own. He knew that when he kissed this girl, and forever wed his unutterable visions to her perishable breath, his mind would never romp again like the mind of God. So he waited, listening for a moment longer to the tuning fork that had been struck upon a star. Then he kissed her. At his lips' touch she blossomed for him like a flower and the incarnation was complete.

FULLER AND MCGEE CASE

Updating Perkins on the novel on 10 September, Fitzgerald reported that he had to 'rewrite practically half of it'.[335] He promised that he would mail the book on 1 October. He put it aside for a week, so he could take a fresh last look at it. There was something niggling him. He sensed that he had left something out, 'some intangible sequence lacking somewhere in the middle'. He was concerned a break in interest there would mean the failure of the book. This 'intangible' piece at the centre of the novel would dominate his thinking for months.

Adding to pressure to complete the book was his dire financial position. He felt obligated to provide the lifestyle that he had promised to Zelda in Montgomery. If she had married one of her other wealthy suiters, she would have been guaranteed a comfortable life, as her parents reminded her. 'I can't reduce our scale of living,' he informed Perkins, 'and I can't stand this financial insecurity.'[336] Each extra week spent on the novel lowered his already diminished capital. 'I'm about broke,' he pleaded to Ober promising to write a story as soon as the novel was complete, and follow up with two more within a month, 'and as you have no doubt already guessed I'm going to ask you for an advance on it.'[337]

More weeks went by without completion. 'My novel goes to you with a long letter within five days,' he assured Perkins during the second week of October. 'This is just a hurried scrawl as I'm working like a dog.'[338] Notwithstanding the pressure, he found time to recommend a young author to his editor, 'This is to tell you about a young man named Ernest Hemingway, who lives in Paris … has a brilliant future … I'd look him up right away. He's the real thing.' Each letter received from France was 'tantalizing' for Perkins who looked forward to receiving the book.[339] 'Mr. Scriber always asks about you,' he reported back. 'We all miss your calls – that's a fact.'

Progress on the novel was interrupted when Ring Lardner and his wife visited the Riviera. Fitzgerald drove them in the little Renault to Cannes, Nice and Monte Carlo. On 19 October, he informed Ober that the last revision of the novel was being typed.[340] Finally, one week later, on 25 October, he sent *The Great Gatsby* manuscript to him, hoping the novel would be serialised in a magazine for a fee of $15,000 followed by publication in April. Looking further ahead, he would refer 'all moving picture bids' he received on the book to him.

He wrote to Perkins that he wouldn't get a night's sleep until he heard his first impression.[341] He was cautiously confident: 'I think that at last I've done something really my own, but how good "my own" is remains to be seen.'[342] He insisted on no signed praise by other authors on the jacket, as he was 'tired of being the author of This Side of Paradise and I want to start over.' He proposed *Gold-hat-*

ted Gatsby as a new title and offered further alternatives over the following weeks, including *On the Road to West Egg*, *Trimalchio in West Egg* and *Trimalchio*. In *Satyricon* by the Roman Petronius, a rich former slave named Trimalchio throws ostentatious parties. He also asked Perkins to send newspaper accounts of the Harvard-Princeton and Yale-Princeton football games.

The Fitzgeralds decided to winter in Rome when Zelda read *Roderick Hudson* by Henry James. It was a strange choice a their previous visit to the eternal city three years earlier had been disappointing, an experience he described in a letter to Edmund Wilson:

> Rome is only a few years behind Tyre and Babylon. The negroid streak creeps northward to defile the nordic race. Already the Italians have the souls of blackamoors. Raise the bars of immigration and permit only Scandinavians, Teutons, Anglo Saxons and Celts to enter … I think its [*sic*] a shame that England and America didn't let Germany conquer Europe.[343]

Italy at least offered the advantage of a better exchange rate against the dollar.[344] They left the Villa Maria to stay in the Hotel Continental in St Raphael before their final departure. Two weeks after sending the manuscript to Perkins, he wrote from the hotel that he was still 'not satisfied' with the middle of the book, which he identified as Chapters 6 and 7. Chapter 6 included the 'repeat the past' section and Chapter 7 a confrontation between Jay Gatsby and Tom Buchanan. He was considering writing 'a complete new scene'.[345]

Perkins was genuinely thrilled to receive the manuscript when it arrived in the mail and replied immediately after his first reading:

> I think the novel is a wonder … it has vitality to an extraordinary degree, and glamour, and a great deal of underlying thought of unusual quality. It has a kind of mystic atmosphere at times that you infused into parts of 'Paradise' … And as for sheer writing, it's astonishing.[346]

After a second reading from an editorial perspective, he believed that Fitzgerald had 'every kind of right to be proud of this book. It is an extraordinary book.'[347]

Perkins did not shrink from his editorial duty. Agreeing there was 'a certain slight sagging in chapters six and seven', he also believed that Gatsby as a character was 'somewhat vague'. While understanding that may have been an artistic intention, he considered it mistaken. He recommended that Gatsby be described as distinctly as the other characters. Agreeing also that the source of Gatsby's wealth should remain mysterious, he suggested that his connection to Wolfsheim be revealed earlier, recommending that he 'might here and there interpolate some phrases, and possible incidents, little touches of various kinds, that would suggest that he was in some active way mysteriously engaged'.

When he received the letter from Perkins, Fitzgerald was staying at the Hotel des Princes in Rome, a small, comfortable, unfashionable but reasonably priced establishment. His first choice of accommodation, the fashionable Hotel Quirinale with its shared entrance to the Opera, had been full of middle-aged English and stale air.[348] His editor's clear understanding of the novel made him 'feel like a million dollars'.[349] His criticisms were 'excellent and most helpful'. Importantly, he told him he knew 'how to fix' Chapters 6 and 7. He commenced a complex restructuring of the entire novel.

Meanwhile, his financial situation deteriorated further. 'Now as to the all devastating question of money ...,' he wrote to his agent. 'I am very broke and will have to rehabilitate myself with three or four short stories, written one after the other.'[350] Three stories would cover the whole winter 'as life is very cheap, of course here in Rome'. He intended to change his ways, 'Then I'm starting another novel. My loafing days are ... over.' Unable to get an advance from Ober until he completed a story, he turned to Perkins again for a financial bailout. 'I've been slow on starting the stories on which I must live,' he pleaded in early December.[351] Scribner cabled $750 bringing the total advanced by the publisher on the novel to $5,000.[352]

Ten years older, Perkins had become a friend and close confidant. His courage, intelligence and thoughtfulness won the respect of an author particularly sensitive to criticism. As Christmas drew near, a melancholy Fitzgerald sent him a long and personal letter. He was 'a bit (not very – not dangerously) stewed'.[353] Rome was cold and gloomy, the hotel was damp and the snores of other guests echoed through thin walls. *Liberty* magazine turned down the novel for serialisation, so he needed to find time and motivation to write short stories to live.[354] 'I now get $2,000 a story,' he revealed, 'but I hate worse than hell to do them.' He thanked him for the money advanced and encouragement, 'I think (for the first time since the Vegetable failed) that I'm a wonderful writer and its [*sic*] your always wonderful letters that help me go on believing in myself.'

His main purpose in writing the letter was to address Perkins' criticism of the vagueness of Gatsby's character: 'I myself didn't know what Gatsby looked like or was engaged in and you felt it.' He was originally modelled 'half unconsciously' on an older man. Fitzgerald had seriously considered dropping Gatsby as the main protagonist: 'my first instinct after your letter was to let him go and have Tom Buchanan dominate the book'. He believed that Tom was the best character he had ever done and one of the 'three best characters in American fiction in the last twenty years, perhaps and perhaps not'.

But he did not give up on his protagonist: 'Gatsby sticks in my heart. I had him for awhile then lost him and now I know I have him again.' He had found a new model for his character, 'after careful searching of the files (of a man's mind here) for the Fuller Magee case, and after having had Zelda draw pictures until her fingers ache I know Gatsby better than I know my own child'.[355]

During the summer of 1923, when Fitzgerald engaged intermittently on the novel, he followed the sensational Fuller and McGee securities fraud case. His Long Island neighbour Edward M. Fuller, a prominent New York stockbroker known for his society connections, was front page news. Fuller's brokerage firm went bankrupt a year earlier for $6,000,000, setting in motion high-profile indictments against him and his business partner Frank McGee.[356]

Arnold Rothstein was implicated in the Fuller McGee case fuelling public interest. The *New York Times* reported on 28 July that he admitted to lending money to their former attorneys. Cool, smiling and evasive, Rothstein than refused to answer questions intending to show he had won $385,000 in bets from Fuller, who had reportedly lost more than $22,000 on one bet on the 1919 World Series.[357] Excitement in the case reached fever-pitch when the wives of the partners, both Broadway musical stars, denied obtaining lavish gifts and insisted they had lost money in the firm's crash.[358] Fuller and McGee were imprisoned in 1927 and paroled within a year. Five years later, Fuller was found with an apparently self-inflicted bullet wound in the head in the Miami house he was about to lose.[359]

Edward M. Fuller became the new model for Gatsby whose criminality is elevated to white collar crime, which is never explicitly stated to maintain the sense of mystery about him. Fitzgerald retains his connection to Wolfsheim but deletes a reference to the Jewish mobster 'dealing in stolen bonds' to separate Gatsby's more glamourous financial crime from his bootlegging and gambling activities.[360] Gatsby accounts for his wealth to Carraway by telling him that he had been in the drug and oil business, and offers him an opportunity in bonds to thank him for arranging the secret meeting with Daisy:

'Why, I thought – why, look here, old sport, you don't make much money, do you?'

'Not very much.' …

'I thought you didn't, if you'll pardon my – you see, I carry on a little business on the side, a sort of side line, you understand. And I thought that if you don't make very much – You're selling bonds, aren't you, old sport?'

'Trying to.'

'Well, this would interest you. It wouldn't take up much of your time and you might pick up a nice bit of money. It happens to be a rather confidential sort of thing.' …

'I've got my hands full,' I said. 'I'm much obliged but I couldn't take on any more work.'

'You wouldn't have to do any business with Wolfsheim.'

Evidently he thought that I was shying away from the 'gonnegtion' mentioned at lunch, but I assured him he was wrong.

As well as remodelling Gatsby, he brought his character to life with more physical descriptions and dialogue. He moved forward the origin story of Jimmy Gatz from the end of the novel and he fixed '1,000 minor corrections … and several more large ones'. During this process, he had to write a story for Ober and ask him for an advance to 'get me out of the hole'.[361] He was revising a second story, a third was at the typist and he was starting a fourth, under such pressure that he offered a prayer to Ober 'that this novel will put me on a financial footing where I won't be such a beggar always I am'. If the novel was not a commercial success, he would be in real trouble. He wrote to Thomas Boyd that he was 'crazy with nervousness'.[362]

Drinking too much, one night he got into a brawl with a taxi driver and a plain-clothes detective resulting in an overnight cell stay and a severe beating which left him sore for some time, later describing the experience as 'just about the rottenest thing that ever happened to me in my life'. The temperature went below three degrees in Rome. He could not stand the cold and was confined to bed for a week with grippe. Zelda underwent a difficult fertility operation leaving her with a lingering infection. Rome's 'thieving waiters' got under his skin. When Ober presented a lucrative offer to write a story for the *Evening Post* on his experience of the city, he turned it down: 'I hate Italy and the Italians so violently that I can't bring myself to write about them for the Post – unless they'd like an article called "Pope Siphilis the Sixth and his Morons" or something like that.'[363]

Plaza Scene

Broke, exhausted and dismally unhappy, Fitzgerald ploughed through the complicated rewrite. He was 'humiliated' to have to wire Ober for another $300 to get through Christmas, noting that if all three stories sold he would be 'out of danger'.[364] His relationship with Zelda became strained and there was 'ill feeling' between the couple.[365] He had a brief flirtation with film star Carmel Myers, whom he met on the spectacular film set of *Ben-Hur: A Tale of the Christ*. At a Christmas party for the movie company, Zelda received the attention of an American journalist. He noted in his diary for December: 'Depression … Movie party … Row in Café … Xmas row …' In a later letter to Zelda, he summed up the period: 'I was really alone with no one I liked in Rome we were dismal.'[366]

When he received the typed proofs of the manuscript from Perkins, he was 'ready to attack it violently'.[367] He sent the first revisions on 24 January instructing the editor not to disclose the plot on the cover: 'Don't give away that Gatsby … is a parvenu or a crook or anything. It's a part of the suspense of the book that all these things are in doubt until the end.'[368] He revealed his loneliness at the end of the letter: 'I miss seeing you, Max, more than I can say.'

The confrontation between Gatsby and Buchanan continued to haunt him. He had tested a number of different scene settings before settling on a suite in the Plaza Hotel on a stifling hot afternoon. Before the revision process commenced, Fitzgerald had explained to Perkins his concerns that the hotel scene 'will never quite be up to mark – I've worried about it too long and I can't quite place Daisy's reaction. But I can improve it a lot … The rest is easy.'[369] He had informed Ober that the book 'has some bad flaws' in Chapters 6 and 7, which he hoped 'to remedy in proof but on the whole I am very proud of it'.[370]

Almost his entire focus was on the Plaza encounter through January, excitedly informing Perkins at the end of the month that the hotel scene 'is now wonderful and that makes the book wonderful'.[371] He expressed his relief to Ober that he had 'spent three extra weeks … clearing up that bum plaza hotel scene and now it's really almost perfect of its kind'.[372] But he spent three more weeks working on the scene, until finally he ran out of time and sent it to Scribner.

'HOLD UP GALLEY FORTY FOR BIG CHANGE', he wired Perkins urgently on the morning of 18 February.[373] At the final moment before printing, he cut, extended and re-wrote whole sections of the confrontation scene marking the changes on the long single-column printer's proof.[374] He followed up the cable with a letter: 'This morning I wired you to hold up the galley … The correction – and God! its [sic] important because in my other revision I made Gatsby look too mean – is enclosed herewith.'

He had finally finished the novel and he was proud of his achievement. 'After six weeks of uninterrupted work the proof is finished,' he wrote to Perkins with the final correction. '... On the whole it has been very successful labor.'[375] He had stuck with Gatsby as his protagonist, bringing him to life and accounting for his money, and he had 'fixed up the two weak chapters'. Perkins replied that Gatsby was 'now most appealing, effective and real, and yet altogether original'.[376] Fitzgerald later credited him for his role in restructuring the novel: 'Max, it amuses me when praise comes in on the "structure" of the book – because it was you who fixed up the structure, not me.'[377]

The last gasp changes made to the plaza confrontation on the final morning are substantial. The set-up of the scene is given more tension. As the group – Gatsby, Tom, Carraway, Daisy and Jordan – prepare to leave Long Island for New York, Tom establishes dominance over Gatsby by making to drive his 'circus wagon' of a car, a suggestion that is 'distasteful' to Gatsby:

'I don't think there's much gas,' he objected.

'Plenty of gas,' said Tom boisterously. He looked at the gauge.

'And if it runs out I can stop at a drugstore. You can buy anything at a drugstore nowadays.'

The last remark is loaded with insinuation. Tom had conducted an investigation into Gatsby's affairs after the party discovering that he was involved in selling alcohol over drugstore counters. Fitzgerald places emphasis on the expression on Gatsby's face:

> A pause followed this apparently pointless remark. Daisy looked at Tom frowning, and an indefinable expression, at once definitely unfamiliar and vaguely recognizable, as if I had only heard it described in words, passed over Gatsby's face.

Fitzgerald left the next section of the text broadly unchanged. Daisy rejects Tom's offer to ride with him in the yellow Rolls Royce, instead choosing to follow with Gatsby in the blue coupé, suggestively walking close to him, touching his coat with her hand. Tom notices, accelerates off first into the oppressive heat and stops at Wilson's garage for gas. The coupé flashes by with a flurry of dust and the flash of a waving hand. Tom learns from Wilson that he plans to take Myrtle west, whether she wants to or not. He suspects an affair, but not with Tom. Myrtle stares at them intently from an upstairs window in the dust-covered garage. Tom feels 'the hot whips of panic. His wife and his mistress, until an hour ago secure and inviolate, were slipping precipitately from his control.' He steps on the accelerator with the double purpose of overtaking Daisy and leaving Wilson behind.

When they arrive at the Plaza and settle into the stifling hot suite to have a drink, the prize fight for Daisy commences. When Tom criticises her for cribbing about the heat, Gatsby comes to her defence: '"Why not let her alone, old sport?" remarked Gatsby. "You're the one that wanted to come to town."'

Tom taunts Gatsby about his speech affectation, '"All this 'old sport' business. Where'd you pick that up?"' Daisy comes to his defence. Fitzgerald amplifies Tom's antagonism in a new section that makes him look stupid. He attempts to shatter Gatsby's claim that he went to Oxford, but his opponent explains he had been there for five months under a programme offered to officers after the war to attend any of the universities in England or France. Daisy smiles faintly and Nick has a renewal of complete faith in his neighbour and wants to slap him on the back. Tom gets everything out in the open in a largely unedited section:

'What kind of a row are you trying to cause in my house anyhow?'
'He isn't causing a row,' Daisy looked desperately from one to the other. 'You're causing a row. Please have a little self-control.'

'Self-control!' repeated Tom incredulously. 'I suppose the latest thing is to sit back and let Mr. Nobody from Nowhere make love to your wife.'

Gatsby excitedly cries out that Daisy does not love Tom, that she *never* loved him, that they loved each other for five years. Tom attacks the claim as impossible because of Gatsby's low social standing:

'You're crazy!' he exploded. 'I can't speak about what happened five years ago, because I didn't know Daisy then – and I'll be damned if I see how you got within a mile of her unless you brought the groceries to the back door.'

Gatsby walks over and stands beside her. He asks Daisy to tell the truth – that she *never* loved Tom. She hesitates. She looks at Jordan and Carraway, 'with a sort of appeal as though she realized at last what she was doing – and as though she had never, all along, intended doing anything at all.' Tom reminds her of good times they had spent together with husky tenderness. His tactic works; she cries out that Gatsby wants too much: 'I did love him once – but I loved you too.' Gatsby is taken aback. Tom lands a line that bites physically. A line that Fitzgerald either said, or wished he had said, to Jozan: '"Why – there's things between Daisy and me that you'll never know, things that neither of us can ever forget."'

Gatsby declares that Daisy *is* leaving Tom. She agrees. Tom has enough of the sparring: "'She's not leaving me!'" Tom's words suddenly leaned down over Gatsby. "Certainly not for a common swindler who'd have to steal the ring he put on her finger.'"

In the original manuscript, the scene effectively finishes here. But Fitzgerald added in a completely new section revealing the extent of Gatsby's criminality and enabling Tom to land a knock-out blow, and ultimately revealing the meaning and purpose of the entire scene:

'I found out what your "drugstores" were.' He turned to us and spoke rapidly. 'He and this Wolfsheim bought up a lot of side-street drugstores here and in Chicago and sold grain alcohol over the counter. That's one of his little stunts. I picked him for a bootlegger the first time I saw him, and I wasn't far wrong.'

'What about it?' said Gatsby politely. 'I guess your friend Walter Chase wasn't too proud to come in on it.'

'And you left him in the lurch, didn't you? You let him go to jail for a month over in New Jersey. God! You ought to hear Walter on the subject of you.'

'He came to us dead broke. He was very glad to pick up some money, old sport.'

'Don't you call me "old sport"!' cried Tom. Gatsby said nothing. 'Walter could have you up on the betting laws too, but Wolfsheim scared him into shutting his mouth.'

That unfamiliar yet recognizable look was back again in Gatsby's face.

'That drugstore business was just small change,' continued Tom slowly, 'but you've got something on now that Walter's afraid to tell me about.'

I glanced at Daisy, who was staring terrified between Gatsby and her husband …

Carraway, as narrator, describes Gatsby's facial reaction to his exposure as a criminal:

Then I turned back to Gatsby – and was startled at his expression. He looked – and this is said in all contempt for the babbled slander of his garden – as if he had 'killed a man.' For a moment the set of his face could be described in just that fantastic way.

The looked 'passed'. The scene is over. Gatsby is beaten. Daisy can't stand the encounter anymore. Tom tells her to go on home with Gatsby. 'Go on. He won't annoy you. I think he realizes that his presumptuous little flirtation is over.' Nervous, and thinking it would steady her, she drives the yellow Rolls Royce into the dusk.

Approaching the ash-heaps and passing Wilson's garage, Myrtle runs out into the road waving her hands and shouting. She thinks it is Tom in the Rolls Royce. Daisy turns toward an oncoming car to avoid her, and losing her nerve, turns back. Gatsby tries to swing the wheel, but it is too late. The 'death car' keeps going and disappears around the bend. Myrtle, instantly killed, lies on the road, all her vitality gone.

Gatsby drops Daisy home intending to take the blame for her, if necessary. Carraway later witnesses Tom and Daisy conspiring together with 'an unmistakable air of natural intimacy'. They escape Long Island with no forwarding address and leave a trail of emotional and physical destruction behind:

> They were careless people, Tom and Daisy – they smashed up things and creatures and then retreated back into their money or their vast carelessness, or whatever it was that kept them together, and let other people clean up the mess they had made …

DEATH OF AN IRISHMAN

'He looked – and this is said in all contempt for the babbled slander of his garden – as if he had "killed a man." For a moment the set of his face could be described in just that fantastic way.'

F. Scott Fitzgerald, *The Great Gatsby*

The scene that bothered Fitzgerald for months is bookended by the expression on Gatsby's face. At the first hint of his exposure, the expression is indefinable, unfamiliar yet recognisable. At the end of the scene, Gatsby looks as if he had 'killed a man'.

Fitzgerald places the words within quotation marks. He makes it clear, not just with extra punctuation, that his meaning is not that Gatsby had taken a life. Firstly, he dismisses any connection to the 'babbled slander' heard by Carraway that Gatsby had killed a man. Secondly, the set on his face is 'fantastic'; it is not meant to be taken literally. Thirdly, the confrontation between Tom and Gatsby never became physical. Finally, Nick is 'startled' at the expression, not shocked, and he continues to be Gatsby's friend. He shakes his hand at their final meeting, shouting back across his lawn, 'They're a rotten crowd. You're worth the whole damn bunch put together.'

During the final revision on that final morning, Fitzgerald added a new line in the chapter following the Plaza scene explaining the impact the encounter had on his protagonist: '"Jay Gatsby" had broken up like glass against Tom's hard malice.'[378]

Again, 'Jay Gatsby' has its own quotation marks. The 'Jay Gatsby' invented by the seventeen-year-old young man, the platonic conception of himself, had shattered on his exposure and the 'long secret extravaganza was played out'. Tom exposed his low social standing, Mr Nobody from Nowhere, fit enough only to bring the 'groceries' to the back door, and he is a 'common' criminal.

But Gatsby has strayed so far that he is no longer James Gatz. And after committing himself to Daisy, he cannot return to the point in his life that was most open to possibility. He cannot fix everything just the way it was before. He cannot recover that something, that some idea of himself, that had gone into loving her. He cannot repeat the past. For that brief moment when that look is on his face, Gatsby realised that he had killed his younger self.

Just months after the novel was published, Fitzgerald explained to John Peale Bishop that Gatsby 'started as one man I knew and then changed into myself'.[379] In an inscription to a first edition of the novel, he wrote that Gatsby's 'original served for a good enough exterior until about the middle of the book he grew thin and I began to fill him with my own emotional life'.[380]

Fitzgerald always struggled to create convincing characters outside himself. Writing *The Great Gatsby* as a purely creative work, one not relying on his own personal experience, proved too much of a challenge. John O'Hara, an author and friend, believed that Fitzgerald was 'more interested in the life, rather than the lives of his protagonists'. He added that the problem with much of his writing was that his characters 'always came back to being Fitzgerald characters in a Fitzgerald world'.[381] Later in life, Scott agreed: 'My characters are all Scott Fitzgerald.'[382]

His closest friends understood the reason for his difficulty with characterisation. At a low point in their relationship, Sara Murphy sent him an affectionate but frank letter. 'I have always told you, you haven't the faintest idea what anybody else but yourself is like.'[383] She criticised him for trampling on other people's feelings, blaming his actions partly on the self-indulgence of his drinking which turned him into someone else, instead of the Scott 'we know, and love, and admire'. Her explanation for his inconsideration was damning. 'It is that you are only thinking of yourself.' Hemingway believed that Fitzgerald started with real people, but failed because 'he knows nothing about them'.[384]

Gatsby is Fitzgerald, and not just from the middle of the novel. Behind the exterior façade of his characterisation lay the author. He disguised his younger self as 'Rudolph Miller' in 'Absolution', likewise he gave Jimmy Gatz a German immigrant heritage, adding a possibly Lutheran faith, and he layered Gatsby with the affectations of Gerlach, the styling of Fleischman and the financial veneer of Fuller. He resented that critics failed to perceive his 'countenance behind Gatsby's mask'.[385]

Fitzgerald, like Gatsby, projected an idealised version of himself, or platonic conception of himself, to society. Tom had only to scratch to reveal Gatsby's shame. Fitzgerald's veneer was equally thin. He rejected his parents as a child in his imagination and as an adult in his writing, and abandoned his Celtic philosophy and Catholicism. His self-invention attempted to conceal his shame at being born of the Irish race. When Fitzgerald wrote that Gatsby looked like he had 'killed a man', he recognised, consciously or not, that he had killed his younger self; the boy who was Irish on both sides. It was the death of an Irishman.

He confessed eight years later and served a bitter sentence.

Confession of Being a Gael

On the day after Myrtle was savagely run over, Gatsby put on his bathing-suit and left word with the butler that if anyone phoned – he was clutching a last hope Daisy would call – word was to be brought to him at the pool. Fitzgerald unleashed his prose talent when Carraway reveals the final action in the Gatsby tale and the author's disillusion:

I have an idea that Gatsby himself didn't believe it would come, and perhaps he no longer cared. If that was true he must have felt that he had lost the old warm world, paid a high price for living too long with a single dream. He must have looked up at an unfamiliar sky through frightening leaves and shivered as he found what a grotesque thing a rose is and how raw the sunlight was upon the scarcely created grass. A new world, material without being real, where poor ghosts, breathing dreams like air, drifted fortuitously about … like that ashen, fantastic figure gliding toward him through the amorphous trees.

A distraught and deranged Wilson discovered that Gatsby was the owner of the yellow car. He finds the house and shoots him in the pool before turning the gun on himself, 'and the holocaust was complete'.

Immediate on sending the revised proofs to Scribner, Fitzgerald and Zelda escaped Rome for the beautiful rugged island of Capri in the Bay of Naples. The move did not work out well, however, and during the first month they had a 'hell of a time' as both fell ill. Zelda was sick in bed in pain for three weeks suffering with colitis or possibly a reaction to her operation. He had also blown the substantial money received for his short stories. 'I don't know whats [*sic*] the matter with me,' he confided in Ober. 'I can't seem to keep out of debt. Whenever I get ahead things like this sickness happen. Such is life.'[386] He wrote more stories 'thick and fast' to make up the deficit and took an advance of $750 from Perkins, swelling his debt to Scribner to over $6,000.

Fitzgerald drank with nervous anxiety in anticipation of the publication date. 'CRAZY ABOUT TITLE "UNDER THE RED WHITE AND BLUE" STOP WHAT WOULD DELAY BE', he wired on 19 March.[387] It was too late. With his artistic reputation and financial security on the line, overcome with 'fears and forebodings', and unable to wait for the cable with the first sales reports, he penned a letter to Perkins from the Hotel Tiberio on 10 April, the day of publication, even though it would not arrive until after the news. He feared women wouldn't like the book because it had no strong female character and critics not like it because it dealt with the rich and not the fashionable rural poor; maybe it wouldn't even wipe out his debt − 'why it will have to sell 20,000 copies even to do that!' And he was still hung up on the Plaza confrontation, 'what should be the strong scene … is hurried and ineffective'[388]

'Reviews Excellent. No data yet on Sales.'[389] Fitzgerald was in Marseilles on his way to Paris after exiting Capri when he received the cable from Perkins. Reading between the lines he wrote to Ober, 'I gather it didn't get off to a flying start.'[390] Perkins was unable to explain why a 'great many of the trade have been very skeptical'. The small size of the book, less than 50,000 words, was a contributing factor.[391] Fitzgerald attributed the disappointing performance to the title and to the absence of an important female character, 'women control the fiction market at present'.[392]

Early reviews were broadly positive, not excellent, and few critics really understood the work. Two weeks after publication, Perkins noted that most of the reviewers 'seem rather to fumble with the book … Of course none of the best people have reviewed yet … who will really understand and grasp it, and so far nobody has done that'.[393] Later reviews were mixed, some notoriously negative. Perkins believed critics could not see that Fitzgerald was a satirist and that he had risen 'above the heads of the multitudes'.[394] Fitzgerald, angry at the 'absolutely stupid and lowsy' critics, vowed that 'Some day they'll eat grass, by God!'[395]

The two print runs, just under twenty-four thousand copies, did not sell out. Fitzgerald received $1,982 in net royalties in the first year, after deducting advances of $4,264. He was far from destitute, however, earning more than $18,000 in total that year, equivalent to over $320,000 today, with the majority of his income, over sixty percent, coming from short stories sold by Ober.

He was proud at having created a work of art, which had received praise in his own literary circle, and though miserable at the prospect of writing more 'cheap' stories, he was already planning a new novel. 'This thing, both the effort and the result have hardened me,' he wrote to Perkins in May, 'and I think now that I'm much better than any of the young Americans without exception.'[396] He later wrote that he 'had dragged the great Gatsby out of the pit of my stomach in a time of misery', but that was now over.[397] So was the failure of *The Vegetable*, the misery of writing stories over the dreary winter on Long Island and the pain of the Jozan affair:

> Then we came to Paris and suddenly I realized that it hadn't all been in vain. I was a success the biggest man in my profession everybody admired me and I was proud I'd done such a good thing. I met Gerald and Sara who took us for friends now and Ernest who was an equal and my kind of an idealist. I got drunk with him on the Left Bank in careless cafés and drank with Sara and Gerald in their garden in St. Cloud.

He confidently wrote to Perkins in September that his new novel 'is going to be great'.[398] And he hit the financial jackpot when Ober sold the *Gatsby* moving picture and theatre rights for $13,500 and $7,764 respectively, swelling his total income from the title to over $32,000. The play opened up to a full house at the Ambassador Theatre on Broadway in February 1926, less than ten months after the publication of the book, receiving favourable reviews and running for the season before going on the road.[399] The silent movie was released in November of that year to reasonable critical response, though the Fitzgeralds thought it 'rotten' and walked out of a cinema in Los Angeles when they saw it the following year.[400] Only the trailer of the first film adaptation survives.

Soon his drinking took control. 'I had developed such an inferiority complex,' he later wrote, 'that I couldn't face anyone unless I was tight.'[401] In drinking parlance, he was a bad and messy drinker with a low tolerance for alcohol, though that expanded through the years. He was disagreeable, mean, rude, quarrelsome and sometimes destructive; the type to lob ashtrays at nearby tables or toss wineglasses over a wall, as he did at a caviar and champagne party hosted by the Murphys, after which they exiled him for three weeks.[402] He later revealed his 'self-disgust when I had put on some unsightly personal show'.[403] Even Hemingway avoided him for a time. Though uncharitable in his later criticism of his friend, he was close to the mark when he observed that Scott was 'fragile Irish instead of tough Irish'.[404] He wrote to Perkins that he had 'gone into that cheap Irish love of defeat, betrayal of himself etc'.[405]

In a 1933 letter to John O'Hara, that he called a 'confession of being a Gael', Fitzgerald revealed his inner demons: the two-cylinder inferiority complex, his intense social self-consciousness and feeling like a parvenu no matter how big his success, and having to continually self-justify when entering new environments.[406]

O'Hara, not yet an established novelist, initiated the confessional correspondence after reading 'More Than Just A House', a Fitzgerald story in the *Saturday Evening Post* about a poor young man named Lew Lowrie 'on his way up'.[407] O'Hara was impressed with Fitzgerald's characterisation and wondered why he did the social climber so well: 'Is it the Irish in you? Must the Irish always have a lot of climber in them?'[408]

O'Hara had a family background similar to Fitzgerald's, except the breeding was on his mother's side. 'Good God! I am the son of a black Irish doctor and a mother who was a Sacred Heart girl,' he blurted out before explaining that his maternal Irish grandmother had married a Pennsylvania Quaker, who converted to Catholicism and had Dutch and English heritage. He expanded that his father was the first doctor in the United States to use oxygen in pneumonia cases and one of the most skilled surgeons in the world. 'But do I have to tell you which side of the family impresses me most?' he asked. 'I doubt it … I go through some cheap shame when the O'Hara side gets too close for comfort.' Incisively, he added, 'If you've had the same trouble, at least you've turned it into a gift … in Lowrie you've done a sort of minor Gatsby.'

O'Hara struck a chord with Fitzgerald who was 'especially grateful' for his letter and, maybe for the first time, he confessed his shame in his Irish heritage and the effect it had on his personality.

I am half black Irish and half old American stock with the usual exaggerated ancestral pretensions. The black Irish half of the family had the money and looked down upon the Maryland side of the family who had, and really had, that certain series of reticences and obligations that go under the poor old shattered word 'breeding' (modern form 'inhibitions'). So being born in that atmosphere of crack, wisecrack and countercrack I developed a two-cylinder inferiority complex.

He still saw himself, like O'Hara, as Irish on one side of the family only. He revealed that no matter what he achieved in life he would always be perceived as a climber.

So if I were elected King of Scotland tomorrow after graduating from Eton, Magdalene, and the Guards, with an embryonic history which tied me to the Plantagenets, I would still be a parvenu … I suppose this is just a confession of being a Gael though I have known many Irish who have not been afflicted by this intense social self-consciousness.

Notwithstanding attending Princeton and belonging to one of its 'snootiest clubs', he had 'an inner necessity of starting my life and my self justification over again at scratch in whatever new environment I may be thrown'.

Three years later, in his novel *Butterfield 8*, O'Hara addressed his own social status issues in 'non-Irish, anti-Catholic' America, when the semi-autobiographical Jimmy Malloy engages with an upper-class girl in a bar:

'People like you make me mad, I mean people like you, people whose families have money and send them to good schools and belong to country clubs and have good cars – the upper crust, the swells …'

'I beg your pardon, but why are you talking about you people, you people, your kind of people, people like you. You belong to a country club, you went to good schools and your family at least *had* money –'

'I want to tell you something about myself that will help to explain a lot of things about me. You might as well hear it now. First of all, I am a Mick. I wear Brooks clothes and I don't eat salad with a spoon and I probably could play five-goal polo in two years, but I am a Mick. Still a Mick …'

'I'm pretty God damn American, and therefore my brothers and sisters are, and yet we're not American. We're Micks, we're non-assimilable, we Micks. We've been here, at least some of my family, since before the Revolution.'

Body of an American

> 'We straggled down quickly through the rain to the cars. Owl-
> eyes spoke to me by the gate.
>
> "I couldn't get to the house," he remarked.
>
> "Neither could anybody else."
>
> "Go on!" He started. "Why, my God! they used to go there by
> the hundreds."
>
> He took off his glasses and wiped them again, outside and in.
>
> "The poor son-of-a-bitch," he said.'
>
> F. Scott Fitzgerald, *The Great Gatsby*

'Owl-eyes' is a minor character who appears in three short scenes in *The Great Gatsby*. Carraway encounters the stout, middle-aged man with enormous owl-eyed spectacles in the library of Gatsby's home during one of his parties, and on the same evening, standing beside the new coupé violently shorn of one wheel. Both scenes are packed with symbolism, as is Gatsby's funeral, where Carraway encounters him for a third time.

Owl-eyes may be all-seeing, a God-symbol, like the giant fading billboard brooding over the valley of the ashes; its gigantic blue eyes looking through enormous yellow spectacles advertising the ophthalmic services of

Doctor T. J. Eckleburg. Or maybe he is just a person with the common decency to show up at the funeral of a man that he once knew. Other than Carraway, servants and the postman from West Egg (the latter without explanation), no one arrived for the service; not Daisy who loved him, not Wolfsheim who made him and not the multitudes that took advantage of his hospitality.

In 1934, *Tender is the Night* was finally published, nine years after *The Great Gatsby*. In the interim period, Fitzgerald, a partially-functioning alcoholic, had to churn out story after story to fund his lifestyle, averaging six a year at over $3,000 dollars each. The novel generated acceptable sales during the depression, though lower than he had hoped, and the highly anticipated book received mixed reviews. 'It has become increasingly plain to me that the very excellent organization of a long book or the finest perceptions and judgment in time of revision do not go well with liquor,' he wrote to the ever-patient Perkins the following year. 'A short story can be written on a bottle, but for a novel you need the mental speed that enables you to keep the whole pattern in your head and ruthlessly sacrifice the sideshows.'

His income declined markedly in 1936 to just $10,000 dollars, earned solely from four stories and nine non-fiction pieces for *Esquire* magazine, including the reflective 'Author's House' and 'An Alcoholic Case'. Unable to cover Zelda's residence at Highland Hospital at an annual cost of over $6,000 dollars, and pay Scottie's tuition, he borrowed heavily from Ober and Perkins (through Scribner and personally), and from John Biggs, his roommate at Princeton, and from his St Paul friend Oscar Kalman.

Owing more than $22,000 and with recurring high financial obligations, Fitzgerald moved to Hollywood in 1937, in the wake of many other writers, securing a lucrative six-month contract with MGM at $1,000 a week, later renewed for $1,250, a small fortune during the depression.[409] Fitzgerald had sojourned twice in Hollywood previously, in 1927 and 1931, though with little success. This time he intended his stay to be different. He sobered up, worked hard, lived modestly and meticulously allocated his weekly cheque in fixed amounts to repay his debts, cover Zelda's hospital stay, pay for Scottie's schooling and build a little holiday fund.

Falling off the wagon in winter 1937, he continued to work hard but to little avail in factory-like Hollywood. Billy Wilder compared him to 'a great sculptor who is hired to do a plumbing job. He did not know how to connect the pipes so the water could flow.'[410] He received his only screen credit for *Three Comrades*, but was angry that producer Joseph Mankiewicz revised much of the screenplay. Mankiewicz went on to win both the Academy Award for Best Director and Best Adapted Screenplay in consecutive years for *A Letter to Three Wives* (1949) and *All About Eve* (1950). When MGM did not renew his contract in December 1938, Fitzgerald took on freelance work. In 1939, he worked briefly as a re-write man on *Gone with the Wind*, though he was not permitted to use any words that did not appear in the novel.[411]

In his spare time and during another attempt at sobriety, he worked on a new novel, *The Last Tycoon*. By the end of 1940, aged forty-four, Scott was more than half way through the book, sober and in a loving relationship with Sheilah Graham, a syndicated Hollywood gossip columnist. Graham wrote about their time together in her memoir, *Beloved Infidel*, made into the 1959 drama film starring Deborah Kerr and Gregory Peck. On the Friday before Christmas, they attended a film preview to celebrate completing a difficult scene of his novel. Rising to leave, he stumbled and gripped the armrest. He made it through the theatre and out to the carpark. Clinging to Sheilah he whispered: 'I suppose people will think I'm drunk.'[412]

On the following morning, after sleeping well, he was cheerful. As a precaution, the doctor was coming later in the day. Sitting in his armchair after lunch, he ate a chocolate bar and made notes on the football team in the *Princeton Alumni Weekly*; he adored the Tigers. Suddenly, he stood up, grabbed the mantelpiece and fell to the floor. One heart can endure only so much.

Scott died believing he was a failure. He could not find his books in stores and copies of *The Great Gatsby* still lay in a corner of Scribner's warehouse. John O'Hara wrote that he 'should have been killed in a Bugatti in the south of France, and not to have died of neglect in Hollywood, a prematurely old little man haunting bookstores unrecognized (as he was the last-but-one time I saw him)'.[413] Laid out in a shabby undertakers in a less salubrious area of Los Angeles, few in Hollywood came to pay their respects; one of those who did, the witty poet and author Dorothy Parker, standing over the body of the once famous author, repeated quietly: 'The poor son-of-a-bitch.'[414]

On Zelda's instruction, the body was taken east for burial with his father's family at St Mary's Cemetery in Rockville, Maryland. However, the Roman Catholic Church would not give its permission because he was not a practising Catholic; there was no absolution or consideration for family. Instead, on a rainy miserable day, he was buried in a cemetery one mile down the road, after a short service by an Episcopalian priest attended by twenty or thirty mourners. Scottie and Ceci Taylor were there, and Gerald and Sara Murphy, and college friends who could make the winter journey, Ludlow Fowler and Judge Biggs. Sheilah Graham did not attend for the sake of propriety, neither did Zelda. In 1975, Scott and Zelda, who died in a horrific fire, were reinterred at the family plot at St Mary's.

There was something inevitable about his destruction. 'Drunk at 20, wrecked at 30, dead at 40,' he wrote in his notebooks. Another entry, albeit under the heading 'Nonsense and Stray Phrases', indicated his state of mind: 'Then I was drunk for many years, and then I died.' He had made an attempt at a Wildean epigram: 'When anyone announces to you how little they drink you can be sure it's a regime they just started.'[415] At one of his lowest points, he wrote to Lois Moran, a Hollywood actress he had an affair with in 1927: 'I believe you are going to be just as happy as it is possible for anybody to be with a dash of the Celt in them.' [416]

Scott had written of Amory Blaine that he did not see himself as a 'strong char'c'ter' and that he knew he lacked 'great animal magnetism'. Growing up in the Midwest, these were traits to be admired and Amory identified them as the 'top things'. Amory also believed he was without courage, perseverance and self-respect. These were qualities and traits that Scott felt he lacked in himself, and which he sought elsewhere. He was attracted to Zelda for her 'courage, her sincerity and her flaming self-respect'. In *This Side of Paradise*, Isabelle has 'intense physical magnetism' and Rosalind 'courage and fundamental honesty'. He blamed his failure to win Ginevra King on his lack of money. But if he had the qualities and traits he lacked, might things have worked out differently, even without wealth? Rosalind chose Dawson Ryder without loving him and not just for his money: 'I respect him, and he's a good man and a strong one.' Although Amory considers Dawson 'a bore, steady and sure of success', he grudgingly agrees that 'he's a good man and a strong one'.

It is easy to picture Scott as a boy in St Paul surrounded by the mercantile McQuillan family listening to conversations praising men deemed of strong character, with courage, perseverance and self-respect. One of those was his grandfather Philip F. McQuillan, but he never met him. Another was James J. Hill. In 1926, in a literary spotlight in the *New Yorker*, he revealed he was research-ing the business leaders of the previous fifty years and that the 'personalities of the major actors, Harriman, Morgan, Hill, is his serious study'. The article described his information on this phase in American history as 'remarkable'.[417] In his later notebooks, he wrote a line in a section for the description of girls for future use: 'Much as the railroad kings of the pioneer West sent their wait-ress sweethearts to convents in order to prepare them for their high destinies'.[418]

Scott had a keen interest in the history of America.

I look out at it – and I think it is the most beautiful history in the world. It is the history of me and of my people. And if I came here yesterday like Sheilah I should still think so. It is the history of all aspiration – not just the American dream but the human dream and if I came at the end of it that too is a place in the line of the pioneers.[419]

He evoked the sense of wonder of the first settlers in closing *The Great Gatsby*, the same sense of unfulfilled wonder he carried in his troubled soul. Carraway, before leaving Long Island and returning to the Midwest, wan-ders down to the beach and sprawls out on the sand:

... there were hardly any lights except the shadowy, moving glow of a ferryboat across the Sound. And as the moon rose higher the inessential houses began to melt away until gradually I became aware of the old island here that flowered once for Dutch sailors' eyes – a fresh, green breast of the new world. Its vanished trees, the trees that had made way for Gatsby's house, had once pandered in whispers to the last and greatest of all human dreams; for a transitory enchanted moment man must have held his breath in the presence of this continent, compelled into an aesthetic contemplation he neither understood nor desired, face to face for the last time in history with something commensurate to his capacity for wonder.

Scott sought acceptance and assimilation as an American from those that *he* believed had a monopoly on Americanism, unlike Judge Daniel F. Cohalan, and others, who refused to accept that his American identity was in any way inferior. On this secure foundation, Cohalan could take pride in his Irish heritage, the good with the bad. During the turbulent summer of 1919, when Scott wrote that Amory Blaine suspected that being Irish was 'rather common', John F. Kennedy was three years old. When writing *The Great Gatsby* on the French Riviera during the summer of 1924, Jack Kelly from Philadelphia, the son of an Irish immigrant father, competing in the Paris Olympic Games, became the first rower to win three gold medals. Five years later, his daughter Grace Patricia Kelly was born. During the 1924 summer games, a team from Ireland as an independent state competed for the first time.

The marriage of Princess Grace into royalty in 1956 and the election of President John F. Kennedy in 1960 mark the final assimilation of the Irish into American social and political society. Princess Grace and her husband, Prince Rainier III of Monaco, made an official state visit to Ireland in 1961. Two years later, John F. Kennedy returned to the homeland of his ancestors as President of the United States of America.

The Great Gatsby is not a story of the American Dream, a term that came into common usage six years after the book was published. How could it be? The protagonist is a criminal who fails to get the girl and is shot. Among other things – including illusion and disillusion in life, imagination and wonder, nostalgia for the past and the pioneering age, the new age of communication, consumption and mobility – the novel is a story of American identity.

The 'Fitzgerald Revival' began when the Council on Books in Wartime distributed free copies of *The Great Gatsby* to American soldiers serving overseas during the Second World War. A critical re-evaluation followed in the 1950s and the work became a core part of American curricula. Stage and film adaptations added to the novel's reputation in popular culture.

The Great Gatsby ends with possibly the most inspiring prose in American literature:

And as I sat there brooding on the old, unknown world, I thought of Gatsby's wonder when he first picked out the green light at the end of Daisy's dock. He had come a long way to this blue lawn, and his dream must have seemed so close that he could hardly fail to grasp it. He did not know that it was already behind him, somewhere back in that vast obscurity beyond the city, where the dark fields of the republic rolled on under the night.

Gatsby believed in the green light, the orgastic future that year by year recedes before us. It eluded us then, but that's no matter – tomorrow we will run faster, stretch out our arms further … And one fine morning –

So we beat on, boats against the current, borne back ceaselessly into the past.

APPENDIX

De Valera in America

Excerpt from *Revolution at the Waldorf: America and the Irish Revolution* by Patrick O'Sullivan Greene.

De Valera had the intellectual and physical stature to fill out the figurehead role of 'President of the Irish Republic' in America. First impressions were of a courteous, frugal and earnest man. He carried an air of integrity and sincerity. Taking up arms in 1916, sentenced to be shot and saved only by 'his American citizenship', his story-book escape from Lincoln Jail, the ease at which he eluded the British and his mysterious arrival in America, all added to his appeal.[420] He drew the working-class Irish to him; he was not a politician (to them) and not of the establishment; he had a genuine Catholic faith.

But de Valera's time in America between June 1919 and December 1920 was marked by strategic mistakes and tactical errors in the conduct of the bond and recognition campaigns, as well as an unnecessary divisiveness. He lacked the interpersonal and management skills to deliver his objectives. His lack of interest and understanding of 'elaborate organisation' – planning, communication, delegation and commercial awareness – resulted in what Edward McSweeney perceived in the bond drive as 'no adequate systematization of the work, and no clear or definite idea of the handling of the mass of detail necessary for such a campaign'.[421] He had attention to detail, a valuable skill, but it was often directed in the wrong direction, and he continually procrastinated, a weakness he recognised in himself. 'If I could only acquire [the] habit of doing things on the spot. I trust I am not too old to improve.'[422]

A remarkable self-belief and self-admitted stubbornness, combined with an almost contradictory insecurity and a jealous streak, was not compatible with inspiring motivation and trust. There was only one voice; compromise and teamwork were not possible. A toxic 'corporate culture' is revealed in the later letters of his earliest supporters in America.

> I am sorry to observe that he is a lamentable failure in meeting delegations or committees or groups in conference. ... In details and methods he appears to most of his visitors as lacking in decision, changeable, unsteady and many men go away feeling they cannot work with him or under him safely.[423] – James K. McGuire.

My experience of him and Harry is that they come to a conference not knowing what they want; have an unconscious
contempt or seem to have such for opinions of others. The
Chief presides and does all the talking … thinks he has
co-operation when he only gets silent acquiescence.[424] –

 – Patrick McCartan.

I would advise you [de Valera] to promptly send someone to
this country who has your confidence, if such a person exists,
and having done so don't constantly interfere with his work.[425]

— James O'Mara.

De Valera survived self-inflicted wounds – the Gazette
interview, the Republican convention and the bond
campaign – through the (sometimes reluctant) support
of those using him to leverage their own agendas, or
because professed loyalty to the 'Irish President' was the
only option without damaging the Irish cause. McCartan
and Maloney leveraged de Valera's presence in America
in their failed liberal takeover of the leadership of the
Irish movement, and the fallout from the dispute enabled
Boland to justify his failed attempt to take control of
Clan-na-Gael. Disgruntled factions challenging the New
York 'clique', and the ambitious quarrelsome 'disturb-
ers' identified by McGuire to Boland, gladly sided with
him in his dispute with Cohalan and Devoy. The Hearst
newspaper organisation pursued its own anti-imperialist
agenda through support of de Valera. The cabinet in

Dublin, with no choice in the matter, had to issue two letters of confidence.

Raising $5.2 million, equivalent to over $75 million today, cannot be dismissed as a failure, but it was a colossal lost opportunity, missing the $10 million target by almost 50 per cent, an opportunity cost of over $70 million today! The launch delays and poor organisation resulted in reputational damage to the Irish movement. Moreover, de Valera's rejection of Edward McSweeney's plan, which had envisaged raising $20 million, had been a mistake. The $10 million target had been achievable as late as February 1920 if, as McGuire noted, they could 'perfect the organisation'. Charles Wheeler had told McGarrity that if unity could be maintained, 'you would get not $10,000,000, but nearer 50,000,000'; while an exaggerated estimate, it is an indication of the opportunity left behind.

Official recognition of the Irish Republic by the United States government was not a realistic objective in the timeframe envisaged by de Valera. Pro-English sentiment in the White House and Congress was too strong to support straight recognition. De Valera's unexpected arrival in America and desire for almost instant success through an appeal to public opinion interfered with the Friends of Irish Freedom's (FOIF's) stepping stone recognition strategy in Washington, nationwide campaign of education and focus on elevating the status of the Irish race (often by challenging an increasing anglicisation of America). The rash decision to establish the American Association for the Recognition of the Irish Republic (AARIR) one month before he left America, after failing to take control of the FOIF through constitutional means, unnecessarily split the Irish movement.

John Devoy perceived de Valera as another in the long line of revolutionaries coming from Ireland who misunderstood America and who believed they knew the country better than those who had been born there or made it their home. Devoy had shown himself capable of working with leaders from Ireland in the past, but he formed a low opinion of de Valera considering him egotistical, insincere and being of poor judgement. Devoy's question to McCartan written on the train from New York could equally have been asked of de Valera. 'Does it ever occur to you that your assumption of infallible judgment is absurd?'[426] He believed de Valera set back the Republican ideal through mixed messaging and the divisions he created in America, and replicated in Ireland.

Devoy merited greater respect for his achievements; not to be harassed to the point of regretting that he had not gone over for Easter Week to be shot with his friends.[427] He found vindication and some solace on his return to Ireland in 1924, but never forgave the man who caused him to be accused of being a traitor to the Irish Republic.

Cohalan was character assassinated in public by McCartan and Maloney and in private by de Valera; accused of capitalising Irish support for personal, social, political and financial gain, and selling his 'priceless birth right for a mess of mephitic pottage'.[428] He became a despot and a malignant defamer, one accused of treason, of plotting, of being part of an underhand conspiracy, of being a dead weight. All this within months of de Valera stating at a National Council meeting that he had received 'every assistance' and always found him 'ready with advice and help.'[429]

Unlike F. Scott Fitzgerald, Cohalan's vocation was the elevation of the Irish race to equality in American society. The establishment of an Irish state with its people free from English colonial rule was crucial to achieving that goal. He fought for Irish independence as an American. De Valera's insecurity prevented him from leveraging Cohalan's record of political achievement and bipartisan access in Washington for the Irish cause. As Devoy asked of McCartan when he first attempted to challenge Cohalan's leadership, 'And who would you put in his place?'[430]

One can only speculate on what could have been achieved in America if the Friends of Irish Freedom had continued its growth trajectory and if de Valera, instead of being the catalyst for its destruction, had used his speaking tours to attract new members. McGuire saw the potential for 5,000 branches across the country. There would have been factional fights, but likely not to the point of being an existential threat to the organisation. The sharp decline in interest in Irish affairs among the Irish in America in the wake of the treaty debate and the civil war might have been averted. There would have been disagreements, but probably not the collapse in membership that the AARIR experienced.

Was the cost of de Valera's time in America the absence of a powerful united organised diaspora providing political, financial and humanitarian support to the new Irish state in the decades that followed?

Select Bibliography

Brown, David S. 2017. *Paradise Lost: A Life of F. Scott Fitzgerald*, Harvard University Press, Cambridge, Massachusetts.

Bruccoli, M. 1973. *As Ever, Scott Fitz: Letters Between F. Scott Fitzgerald and His Literary Agent, Harold Ober, 1919–1940*, Woburn Press, United Kingdom.

Bruccoli, M. 1978. *The Notebooks of F. Scott Fitzgerald*, University of Michigan, Michigan.

Bruccoli, M. 1980. *Correspondence of F. Scott Fitzgerald*, Random House, New York.

Bruccoli, M. 1994. *F. Scott Fitzgerald: A Life in Letters*, Charles Scribner's Sons, New York, Kindle Edition.

Bruccoli, M. 2002. *Some Sort of Epic Grandeur: The Life of F. Scott Fitzgerald*, Second Edition, University of South Carolina Press, Columbia.

Burke, M. 2022. *Race, Politics, and Irish America, A Gothic History*, Oxford University Press, Oxford.

Carroll, F. 2002. *Money for Ireland: finance, diplomacy, politics, and the first Dáil Éireann loans, 1919–1936*, Praeger, London.

Carroll, F. 1969. 'American Opinion on the Irish Question 1910–1923', thesis for the degree of Doctor of Philosophy, Trinity College, Dublin.

Churchwell, S. 2013. *Careless People: Murder, Mayhem and the Invention of The Great Gatsby*, Little, Brown Book Group, Boston.

Creel, G. 1947. *Rebel at Large: Recollections of Fifty Crowded Years*, G.P. Putnam's Sons, New York.

Doorley, M. 2005. *Irish-American Diaspora Nationalism, The Friends of Irish Freedom, 1916-1935*, Four Courts Press, Dublin.

Doorley, M. 2019. *Justice Daniel Cohalan 1865 – 1946, American Patriot and Irish-American Nationalist*, Cork University Press, Cork.

Eble, K.E. 1973. *F. Scott Fitzgerald: A Collection of Criticism edited by Kenneth E. Eble*, Mcgraw-Hill, New York.

Fitzpatrick, D. 2003. *Harry Boland's Irish Revolution*, Cork University Press, Cork.

Fitzgerald, Z. 1932. *Save Me the Waltz*, Charles Scribner's Sons, New York.

Golway, J. 2015. *John Devoy & America's Fight for Ireland's Freedom*, Merrion Press, Dublin.

Kruse, H.H. 2014. *F. Scott Fitzgerald at Work: The Making of 'The Great Gatsby'*, University of Alabama Press, Alabama.

Kuehl, J. & Bryer, J. 1971. *Dear Scott, Dear Max: The Fitzgerald-Perkins Correspondence*, Charles Scribner's Sons, New York.

Lavelle, P. 2011. *James O'Mara: The Story of an Original Sinn Féiner*, Clonmore & Reynolds, Dublin.

Leslie, S. 1917. *The Irish Issue in its American Aspects*, Charles Scribner's Sons, New York.

Leslie, S. 1917. *The End of a Chapter*, Charles Scribner & Sons, New York.

Lynch, D. 1930–1939. *History of the Friends of Irish Freedom*, unpublished.

McCartan, P. 1932. *With De Valera in America*, Borodino Books, New Zealand.

McCullagh, D. 2017. *De Valera: Rise (1882–1932)*, Volume 1, Gill Books, Dublin.

McGough, E. 2013. *Diarmuid Lynch: A forgotten Irish patriot*, Mercier Press, Cork.

Mellow, James R. 1984. *Invented Lives: F. Scott and Zelda Fitzgerald*, Houghton Mifflin, Boston.

Milford, N. 1970. *Zelda: A Biography*, Harper and Row, New York.

O'Doherty, K. 1957. *Assignment: America: De Valera's mission to the United States*, De Tanko Publishers, New York.

Sklar, R. 1967. *F. Scott Fitzgerald: The Last Laocoön*, Oxford University Press, New York.

Stubbs, T. 2017. *American Literature and Irish culture, 1910–55: The politics of enchantment*, Manchester University Press, Manchester.

Talbot, H. 1923. *Michael Collins' Own Story*, Hutchinson, London.

Tansill, C. 1957. *America and the Fight for Irish Freedom*, Devin Adair Co., New York.

Turnbull, A. 1963. *The Letters of F. Scott Fitzgerald*, Charles Scribner's Sons, New York.

Turnbull, A. 1962. *Scott Fitzgerald*, Charles Scribner's Sons, New York.

West, J.L.W. 2006. *The Perfect Hour: The Romance of F. Scott Fitzgerald and Ginevra King*, Random House, New York.

West, J.L.W. 2014. *Trimalchio: An Early Version of The Great Gatsby*, edited with an Introduction by J.L.W. West III, Charles Scribner's Sons, New York.

West, J.L.W. 2018. *The Great Gatsby F. Scott Fitzgerald*, edited by J.L.W. West, III, Cambridge University Press, Cambridge.

ENDNOTES

1   **Prologue: North and South**

1   James L. West, *The Perfect Hour: The Romance of F. Scott Fitzgerald and Ginevra King, His First Love* (Random House, 2007).

2   *Chicago Tribune*, 13 April 1877, p. 2.

3   *Star Tribune*, 10 July 1875, p. 3; 13 July 1875, p. 3.

4   *Star Tribune*, 4 August 1875; *St. Cloud Journal*, 5 August 1875.

5   *Star Tribune*, 3 May 1877, p. 3.

6   S. Donaldson, *Fool for Love: F. Scott Fitzgerald* (University of Minnesota Press, Minnesota, 2012); Lawrence A. Martin, 'Summit Avenue, Architecture Notes' (2001).

7   Gravestone of Mary Fitzgerald, Old Saint Mary's Catholic Church Cemetery, www.findagrave.com.

8   *Galena Daily Gazette*, 12 April 1877.

9   C.C. Andrews, *History of St. Paul, Minn., with illustrations and biographical sketches of some of its prominent men and pioneers* (D. Mason & Co., 1890); *The Saint Paul Globe*, 31 December 1879, p. 2.

10   *Chicago Tribune*, 13 April 1877, p. 2.

11   André Le Vot, *F. Scott Fitzgerald: A Biography*, trans. William Bryon (New York: Doubleday, 1983), p. 8, quoted in David S. Brown, *Paradise Lost: A Life of F. Scott Fitzgerald* (Harvard University Press, Cambridge, Massachusetts, 2017).

12   *The Saint Paul Globe*, 10 June 1888, p. 19.

13   *The Guardian*, 'One blow after another ...', 18 September 2007, an edited version of M. Mok, 'The Other Side of Paradise, Scott

Fitzgerald, 40, Engulfed in Despair', first published in the *New York Post*, 25 September 1936.

14   *Ibid.*

15   F. Scott Fitzgerald (hereafter FSF) to John O'Hara, 18 July 1933, in M.J. Bruccoli, *F. Scott Fitzgerald: A Life in Letters* (Charles Scribner & Sons, New York, 1994).

Part 1

This Side of Paradise

Blood of Some Potentiality

16   *The Guardian*, 'One blow after another ...', 18 September 2007.

17   *Ibid.*

18   M.J. Bruccoli, *Some Sort of Epic Grandeur: The Life of F. Scott Fitzgerald*, 2nd ed. (University of South Carolina Press, Columbia, 2002).

19   FSF Notebooks, no. 1610, M.J. Bruccoli, *The Notebooks of F. Scott Fitzgerald* (University of Michigan, Michigan, 1978).

20   Donaldson, *Fool for Love* (2012).

21   Bruccoli, *Some Sort of Epic Grandeur*, (2002); *The Guardian*, 'One blow after another ...', 18 September 2007.

22   FSF, 'The Death of My Father', *The Princeton University Library Chronicle*, Summer 1951.

23   FSF Ledger, Transcript, January 1909, University of South Carolina.

24   Minnesota Historical Society, www.mnhs.org.

25   *Chicago Tribune*, 7 September 1888, p. 1.

26   A. Mizener, *The Far Side of Paradise: A Biography of F. Scott Fitzgerald* (Houghton Mifflin, Boston, 1965).

27   Donaldson, *Fool for Love* (2012).

28   Bruccoli, *Some Sort of Epic Grandeur* (2002).

29   FSF, 'Author's House', *Esquire*, July 1936.

30 FSF, *This Side of Paradise* (Charles Scribner's Sons, New York, 1920).

31 FSF, 'The Death of My Father', *The Princeton University Library Chronicle*, Summer 1951.

Celtic Seed

32 Brown, *Paradise Lost* (2017).

33 *The Saturday Evening Post*, 'The Freshest Boy', 28 July 1928.

34 FSF, 'My Lost City', in E. Wilson (ed.) *The Crackup* (New Directions, New York, 1945).

35 FSF Ledger, Transcript, January 1912, University of South Carolina.

36 Brown, *Paradise Lost* (2017).

37 FSF Ledger, Transcript, July 1912, University of South Carolina.

38 Mizener, *The Far Side of Paradise* (1965).

39 FSF, *This Side of Paradise* (1920).

40 FSF, *This Side of Paradise* (1920).

41 Brown, *Paradise Lost* (2017).

42 FSF Ledger, Transcript, April 1913, University of South Carolina.

43 FSF, *This Side of Paradise* (1920).

44 'Homage to the Victorians', *New York Tribune*, 14 May 1922, review of Shane Leslie's *The Oppidan*, in Judith Baughman, *F. Scott Fitzgerald on Authorship* (University of South Carolina Press, Columbia, 1996).

45 *Ibid*.

46 *Ibid*.

47 *Ibid*.; FSF, *This Side of Paradise* (1920).

48 See FSF to Max Perkins, 4 September 1919, in Bruccoli, *A Life in Letters* (1994).

49 A. Regan, *Irish in Minnesota* (Minnesota Historical Society Press, 2009).

50   S. Leslie, *The Irish Issue in its American aspects* (Charles Scribner's Sons, New York, 1917).

51   J. Golway, *John Devoy & America's Fight for Ireland's Freedom* (Merrion Press, Dublin, 2015), pp. 117 and 140.

52   A. Turnbull, *Scott Fitzgerald* (Charles Scribner's Sons, New York, 1962).

53   FSF, *This Side of Paradise* (1920).

54   FSF Ledger, Transcript, June 1913, University of South Carolina.

55   *Ibid*.

Spires and Gargoyles

56   FSF, *This Side of Paradise* (1920).

57   *Ibid*.

58   *Ibid*.

59   J. Meyers, *Scott Fitzgerald: A Biography* (Harper Collins, New York, 1994).

60   FSF to Scottie Fitzgerald, 3 August 1940, in Bruccoli, *A Life in Letters* (1994).

61   Donaldson, *Fool for Love* (2012).

62   Bruccoli, *Some Sort of Epic Grandeur* (2002).

63   E. Wilson, *A Prelude* (Farrar, Straus & Giroux, New York, 1967), p.67, quoted in Bruccoli, *Some Sort of Epic Grandeur* (2002).

64   Bruccoli, *Some Sort of Epic Grandeur* (2002).

65   *Louisville Post*, quoted in Brown, *Paradise Lost* (2017).

66   *College Humor* (December 1927), quoted in Donaldson, *Fool for Love* (2012).

67   FSF Ledger, Transcript, March 1915, University of South Carolina.

68   'All his life he would play the clown, when he found himself in a social situation that he felt he could not handle', Bruccoli, *Some Sort of Epic Grandeur* (2002); 'an inner necessity of starting my life

and my self-justification over again at scratch in whatever new environment I may be thrown', FSF to John O'Hara, 18 July 1933, in Bruccoli, *A Life in Letters* (1994).

69   FSF to Annabel Fitzgerald, *c*. 1915, in Bruccoli, *A Life in Letters* (1994); M.J. Bruccoli, *Correspondence of F. Scott Fitzgerald* (Random House, New York, 1980).

70   FSF Ledger, Transcript, May 1915, University of South Carolina.

71   Bruccoli, *Some Sort of Epic Grandeur* (2002).

72   FSF Ledger, Transcript, September 1915, University of South Carolina.

73   FSF, 'Pasting It Together', *Esquire*, March 1936.

74   Bruccoli, *Some Sort of Epic Grandeur* (2002).

75   Brown, *Paradise Lost* (2017).

Poor Boys, Rich Girls

76   FSF Ledger, Transcript, December 1915, University of South Carolina; Minnesota Historical Society, www.mnhs.org.

77   FSF Notebooks, no. 1378, Bruccoli, *The Notebooks of F. Scott Fitzgerald* (1978).

78   Ginevra King to FSF, 24 March 1915, in R.R. Bleil, 'Temporarily Devotedly Yours: The Letters of Ginevra King to F. Scott Fitzgerald' (unpublished PhD dissertation, Pennsylvania State University, 2008).

79   Ginevra King to FSF, 1915, in Brown, *Paradise Lost* (2017).

80   FSF Ledger, Transcript, 1919–38, June 1915, University of South Carolina; Jackson Upperco, 'That's Entertainment!' blog, 25 July 2016, https://jacksonupperco.com/2016/07/page/3/.

81   FSF Ledger, Transcript, June 1915, University of South Carolina.

82   FSF Ledger, Transcript, August 1915, University of South Carolina.

83   The story, 'A Perfect Hour', does not survive. J. West, *The Perfect Hour: The Romance of F. Scott Fitzgerald and Ginevra King* (Random House, New York, 2005) quoted in Brown, *Paradise Lost* (2017); M. Noden, 'F. Scott Fitzgerald's First Love', *Princeton Alumni Weekly*, 1978.

84   FSF Ledger, Transcript, June 1916, University of South Carolina.

85   Brown, *Paradise Lost* (2017).

86   Donaldson, *Fool for Love* (2012).

87   FSF Ledger, Transcript, August 1916, University of South Carolina.

88   Ginevra King to FSF, 29 January 1915, in Bleil, 'Temporarily Devotedly Yours' (2008).

89   There is some dispute that King made the statement, but it was significant enough for FSF to record it beside 'beautiful Billy Mitchell'.

90   Ginevra King Pirie to Arthur Mizener, 7 November 1947, Arthur Mizener Papers Princeton, in Brown, *Paradise Lost* (2017).

91   'Love Notes Drenched in Moonlight; Hints of Future Novels in Letters to Fitzgerald', *New York Times* (hereafter *NYT*), 8 September 2003.

Rise of the Celt

92   FSF Ledger, Transcript, February 1917, University of South Carolina.

93   Bruccoli, *Some Sort of Epic Grandeur* (2002).

94   FSF, *This Side of Paradise* (1920).

95   FSF Ledger, Transcript, February 1917, University of South Carolina.

96   FSF, *This Side of Paradise* (1920).

97   FSF to Cecila Delihant Taylor, 10 June 1917, in R. Sklar, *F. Scott Fitzgerald: The Last Laocoön* (Oxford University Press, New York, 1967).

98   *Nassau Literary Magazine*, vol. 73, no. 2, 1 May 1917.

99   Golway, *John Devoy & America's Fight for Ireland's Freedom* (2015);
        F.M. Carroll, *American Opinion and the Irish Question* (St Martin's
        Press, New York, 1978).

100   FSF, *This Side of Paradise* (1920).

101   Oscar Fingal O'Flahertie Wills Wilde.

Princeton Patriot

102   John Quinn interview with Balfour, Quinn Papers, National
        Library of Ireland (hereafter NLI), MS 1751.

103   Golway, *John Devoy & America's Fight for Ireland's Freedom* (2015).

104   *NY Evening Post*, 25 May 1917, 2 June 1917, p. 1, *Gaelic American*:
        Digital Library, Villanova University (hereafter *GA*).

105   E. Butler, *The Irish Times*, 17 February 2017.

106   Bruccoli, *Some Sort of Epic Grandeur* (2002).

107   President Wilson to Lansing, letter, 10 April 1917, in C. Tansill,
        America and the Fight for Irish Freedom (Devin Adair Co., New York,
        1957), p. 365.

108   Leslie, *The Irish issue in its American aspects* (1917).

109   See Father Fay to FSF, 22 August 1917, in Bruccoli, *Some Sort of
        Epic Grandeur* (2002).

110   FSF to Cecelia Taylor, 10 June 1917, in A. Turnbull, *The Letters of
        F. Scott Fitzgerald* (Charles Scribner's Sons, New York, 1963).

111   FSF to Edmund 'Bunny' Wilson, 'Fall' 1917, in Turnbull, *The
        Letters* (1963); FSF to Edmund Wilson, 10 January 1918, in Bruccoli,
        A Life in Letters (1994).

112   FSF to Edmund 'Bunny' Wilson, 26 September 1917, in Turnbull,
        The Letters (1963).

Red Scare

113   *Ibid.*

114   *Ibid.*

115   *Ibid.*

116   FSF to Edmund 'Bunny' Wilson, 'Fall' 1917, in Turnbull, *The Letters* (1963).

117   FSF to Edmund 'Bunny' Wilson, 26 September 1917, in Turnbull, *The Letters* (1963).

118   Father Fay to FSF, 22 August 1917, in Bruccoli, *Some Sort of Epic Grandeur* (2002).

119   FSF to Edmund 'Bunny' Wilson, 'Fall' 1917, in Turnbull, *The Letters* (1963).

120   *Ibid.*

121   *Ibid.*

122   FSF to Shane Leslie, 4 February 1918, in Bruccoli, *A Life in Letters* (1994).

123   FSF to Edmund 'Bunny' Wilson, 'Fall' 1917, in Turnbull, *The Letters* (1963).

124   *NYT*, 3 November 1917, p. 4.

125   *NYT*, 6 October 1917, p. 11.

126   *NYT*, 16 March 1918, p. 8.

127   Dr Michael Doorley, Cohalan biographer, sourced the original document in the German diplomatic archives, along with several letters from Cohalan to Von Bernstorff. See M. Doorley, *Justice Daniel Cohalan 1865–1946, American Patriot and Irish-American Nationalist* (Cork University Press, Cork, 2019), p. 85.

128   Leslie, *The Irish issue in its American aspects* (1917).

129   *NYT*, 15 October 1917, p. 4.

130   *The Sun*, 22 October 1917, p. 5, NY State Historic Newspapers, https://nyshistoricnewspapers.org/.

The Beginning and End of Everything

131   FSF to 'Mother', 14 November 1917, in Bruccoli, *A Life in Letters* (1994).

132   FSF to Edmund 'Bunny' Wilson, 10 January 1918, in Bruccoli, *A Life in Letters* (1994).

133   Fitzgerald, 'Who's Who-and Why', *Afternoon of an Author* (Simon & Schuster, New York, 1987), p. 84, quoted in S. Kunitz (ed.), *Living Authors: A book of biographies* (H.W. Wilson Company, New York, 1931), p. 128, via Meyers, *A Biography* (1994).

134   Bruccoli, *Some Sort of Epic Grandeur* (2002).

135   Turnbull, *Scott Fitzgerald* (1962).

136   FSF to Edmund 'Bunny' Wilson, 10 January 1918, in Bruccoli, *A Life in Letters* (1994).

137   Editor's note to letter from Shane Leslie to FSF, 11 May 1918, p.29, in Bruccoli, *Correspondence of F. Scott Fitzgerald* (1980).

138   FSF to Shane Leslie, 8 May 1918, in Bruccoli, *A Life in Letters* (1994).

139   Fitzgerald, Z., *Save Me the Waltz* (Charles Scribner's Sons, New York, 1932).

140   FSF Ledger, Transcript, September 1918, University of South Carolina.

141   FSF to Isabelle Amorous, 26 February 1920, in Bruccoli, *Correspondence of F. Scott Fitzgerald* (1980).

142   Bruccoli, *Some Sort of Epic Grandeur* (2002).

143   N. Milford, *Zelda: A Biography* (Harper and Row, New York, 1970).

144   *Ibid.*

145   Turnbull, *Scott Fitzgerald* (1962); Milford, *Zelda* (1970); Fitzgerald, Z., *Save Me the Waltz* (1932).

146   Ginevra King to FSF, July 1918, in Brown, *Paradise Lost* (2017).

147   FSF, *This Side of Paradise* (1920).

148   FSF, 'Pasting It Together' (1936).

149   FSF Ledger, Transcript, 1919–38, University of South Carolina, January 2017.

150   Bruccoli, *Correspondence of F. Scott Fitzgerald* (1980).

151   Roger Burlingame, *Of Making Many Books: A Hundred Years of Reading, Writing and Publishing* (Charles Scribner's Sons, New York, 1946), quoted in Brown, *Paradise Lost* (2017).

152   FSF to Shane Leslie, *c*. January 1918, in Bruccoli, *A Life in Letters* (1994).

153   Bruccoli, *Correspondence of F. Scott Fitzgerald* (1980).

154   Bruccoli, *Some Sort of Epic Grandeur* (2002).

155   Mizener, *The Far Side of Paradise* (1965).

156   FSF to Ruth Sturtevant, 4 December 1918, in Turnbull, *The Letters* (1963).

157   FSF to Isabelle Amorous, 26 February 1920, in Bruccoli, *Correspondence of F. Scott Fitzgerald* (1980).

Breaking Point

158   FSF to Shane Leslie, 13 January 1919, in Bruccoli, *A Life in Letters* (1994).

159   Shane Leslie to FSF, 23 January 1919, in Bruccoli, *Correspondence of F. Scott Fitzgerald* (1980).

160   FSF to Shane Leslie, Jan.–Feb. 1919, in Bruccoli, *A Life in Letters* (1994).

161   FSF to Zelda Fitzgerald, after 22 February, in Bruccoli, *A Life in Letters* (1994).

162   FSF, *My Lost City: Personal Essays, 1920–1940* (Cambridge University Press, Cambridge, 2005).

163   'Who's Who', *Saturday Evening Post*, 18 September 1920, via Mizener,
         The Far Side of Paradise (1965).

164   Wire from FSF to Zelda Fitzgerald, 22 March 1919, in Bruccoli,
         Correspondence of F. Scott Fitzgerald (1980); wire from FSF to Zelda
         Fitzgerald, *c*. 14 April 1919, in Bruccoli, *Correspondence of F. Scott
         Fitzgerald* (1980); Zelda Fitzgerald to FSF, April 1919, in Bruccoli,
         Correspondence of F. Scott Fitzgerald (1980).

165   Zelda Fitzgerald to FSF, Spring 1919, in Bruccoli, *Correspondence of
         F. Scott Fitzgerald* (1980).

166   Mizener, *The Far Side of Paradise* (1965).

167   *Ibid*.

168   FSF, *My Lost City* (2005).

169   *Ibid*.

170   Mizener, *The Far Side of Paradise* (1965).

171   FSF, 'Pasting It Together' (1936).

172   FSF to Ruth Sturtevant, 24 June 1919, in Turnbull, *The Letters*
         (1963).

173   FSF, *This Side of Paradise* (1920).

174   *Ibid*.

175   FSF to Edmund Wilson, 15 August 1919, in Bruccoli, *A Life in
         Letters* (1994).

176   **Coca-Cola and Cigarettes**

         Mizener, *The Far Side of Paradise* (1965).

177   FSF to Frances Turnbull, 9 November 1938, in Bruccoli, *A Life in
         Letters* (1994).

178   FSF to Perkins, 26 July 1919, in Bruccoli, *A Life in Letters* (1994).

179   Max Perkins to FSF, 28 July 1919, in J. Kuehl and J. Bryer, *Dear
         Scott, Dear Max: The Fitzgerald-Perkins correspondence* (Charles Scribner's
         Sons, New York, 1971).

180   Mizener, *The Far Side of Paradise* (1965).

181   *Ibid.*

182   Max Perkins to FSF, 16 September 1919, in Kuehl and Bryer,
       Dear Scott, Dear Max (1971).

'I Know Myself, but That is All'

183   FSF to The Booksellers Convention, early April 1920, in Turnbull,
       The Letters (1963).

184   FSF, 'Pasting It Together' (1936).

185   John Biggs Jr., 'Fitzgerald in Wilmington – The Great Gatsby at
       Bay' (Wilmington) *Sunday Bulletin*, 6 January 1974, p. 9; John D.
       McMaster, 'As I Remember Scott', *Confrontation*, Issue 7, 1973,
       Long Island University, in Brown, *Paradise Lost* (2017).

186   Donaldson, *Fool for Love* (2012).

187   FSF to Anne Ober, 4 March 1938, in Bruccoli, *A Life in Letters*
       (1994).

Return of the Native

188   H. Talbot, *Michael Collins' own story* (Hutchinson, London, 1923).

189   G. Creel, *Rebel at large: Recollections of fifty crowded years* (G.P. Putnam's
       Sons, New York, 1947).

190   *NYT*, 24 June 1919, p. 1.

191   *NYT*, 25 June 1919, p. 4.

192   O'Doherty, K., *Assignment: America: De Valera's mission to the United
       States* (De Tanko Publishers, New York, 1957), p. 43; Sean Nunan,
       Capuchin Annual, 1970, p. 238.

193   *NYT*, 22 June 1919, p. 12.

194   *Ibid.*

195   *NYT*, 25 June 1919, p. 4.

196   *The Brooklyn Daily Eagle*, 25 June 1919, p. 2.

197   *NYT*, 24 June 1919, p. 4.

198   *NYT*, editorial, 25 June, p. 18.

199   O'Hegarty to de Valera, 8 June 1920, National Archives of Ireland (hereafter NAI), DE 2/245, 081.

200   Department of An Taoiseach, 'Information re. Russian Jewels given as security for loan made by Irish Government in 1920', Bureau of Military History, 372.

201   Lynch, Diarmuid, *The IRB and the 1916 Insurrection*, F. O'Donoghue (ed.) (Mercier Press, Cork, 1957), quoted in McGough, E., *Diarmuid Lynch: A forgotten Irish patriot* (Mercier Press, Cork, 2013).

202   E.L. Woodward and R. Butler, *Documents on British Foreign Policy 1919–1939*, 1st series, vol. 5: 1919 (Her Majesty's Stationery Office, London, 1954).

203   D. Lynch, *History of the Friends of Irish Freedom* (unpublished, 1930–39).

204   *GA*, 13 September 1919, p. 1.

205   FSF Ledger, Transcript, June 1919, University of South Carolina; J.R. Mellow, *Invented lives: F. Scott and Zelda Fitzgerald* (Houghton Mifflin, Boston, 1984).

206   40,000 (*NYT*, 30 June 1919, p. 4); 'at least 50,000' (*Boston Globe*); 70,000 (*Irish Press*, 12 July 1919).

207   British Pathé silent newsreel with the intertitle, 'Boston Mass. Éamon De Valera, "President of the Irish Republic" is touring America raising funds for "Sinn Fein"', https://youtu.be/G8ljyohXLv0.

208   *GA*, 12 July 1919, p. 1.

209   *NYT*, editorial, 1 July 1919, p. 15.

210   *NYT*, 5 July 1919, p. 5.

211   *NYT*, 2 July 1919, p. 5; 3 July 1919, p. 4.

212   *Minneapolis Journal*, 6 July 1919.

213 Margaret A. Brucia, *Daisy Chanler, Father Sigourney Fay & F. Scott Fitzgerald* (The Gotham Center for New York City History, 2018).

214 S. Leslie, *The End of a Chapter* (Charles Scribner's Sons, New York, 1917).

215 Tansill, *America and the Fight for Irish Freedom* (1957).

Rancid Accusations

216 *Irish Times*, 14 July 1919; *The Times*, 14 July 1919; *New York Times*, 13 July 1919.

217 Lynch, *History of the Friends of Irish Freedom* (1930–39).

218 F.M. Carroll, 'The American Commission on Irish Independence and the Paris Peace Conference of 1919', *Irish Studies in International Affairs*, vol. 2, no. 1 (1985), pp. 103–18.

219 F. Carroll, 'American Opinion on the Irish Question 1910–1923' (unpublished PhD thesis, Trinity College, Dublin, 1969), p. 49.

220 Senate Foreign Relations Committee hearing, 30 August 1919, quoted in *NYT*, 31 August 1919.

221 *GA*, 20 September 1919, p. 6.

222 Henry White to Senator Cabot Lodge, Carroll, 'American Opinion on the Irish Question' (1969), p. 40.

223 Sean T. O'Kelly to Dublin, 15 June 1919, quoted in Documents on Irish Foreign Policy, www.difp.ie.

224 *NYT*, 31 August 1919, p. 1.

225 Carroll, 'American Opinion on the Irish Question' (1969), p. 40.

226 *Ibid.*

227 *NYT*, 13 July 1919, p. 1.

228 *NYT*, 28 June 1919, p. 6.

229 Shane Leslie to FSF, 23 January 1919, in Bruccoli, *Correspondence of F. Scott Fitzgerald* (1980).

230   Newsletter of the Irish National Bureau, Washington, Issue no. 2, 18 July 1919, Lynch Family Archives.

231   Diary of Sir Horace Curzon Plunkett, 12 January 1923, NLI, transcribed, annotated and indexed by Kate Targett.

232   Professor C.H. Oldham, 'The public finances of Ireland', paper read to the Statistical and Social Enquiry Society of Ireland, 23 January 1920.

233   *GA*, 13 September 1919, p. 1.

234   Tomás Ó Riordán, notice on C.E. Trevelyan, *CELT Multitext Project in Irish History*, National University of Ireland, Cork, www.ricorso.net.

235   *Le Journal* (Paris), 23 January 1920, cited in D. Macardle, *The Irish Republic* (Corgi, London, 1968), p. 308.

236   Diary of Sir Horace Curzon Plunkett, 12 July 1919, NLI.

237   *NYT*, 16 January 1919, p. 11; *NYT* 23 February 1919, S36.

Stigma

238   Lynch, *History of the Friends of Irish Freedom* (1930–39).

239   *NYT*, 22 October 1919, p. 3.

240   D. Cohalan, *Freedom of the Seas* (Friends of Irish Freedom, New York, 1919).

241   Doorley, *Justice Daniel Cohalan* (2019), pp. 20–23; 'Judge Daniel F. Cohalan & The Courtmacsherry Connection', Courtmacsherry & Barryroe History Group, www.courtmacsherrybarryroe history.com/judge-daniel-f-coholan–the-courtmacsherry-connection.html

242   FSF, *This Side of Paradise* (1920).

243   Doorley, *Justice Daniel Cohalan* (2019), p. 23.

244   White Anglo-Saxon Protestant.

245   Doorley, *Justice Daniel Cohalan* (2019), p. 151.

246   Lynch, *History of the Friends of Irish Freedom* (1930–39).

247   *GA*, 12 July 1919, p. 1.

248   *NYT*, 22 December 1919, p. 3.

249   M.J. Sproule, *Propaganda and Democracy: The American Experience of Media and Mass Persuasion* (Cambridge University Press, 1997); *NYT*, 22 December 1919, p. 3.

250   *NYT*, 13 July 1919, p. 22.

251   *NYT*, 14 July 1919, p. 13.

'But I Haven't Any People'

252   'The Literary Spotlight', *The Bookman* literary journal, March 1922, University of California, via Hathi Trust.

253   FSF to Edmund Wilson, January 1922, in Bruccoli, *A Life in Letters* (1994).

254   FSF to Edmund Wilson, late 1920, in Bruccoli, *Correspondence of F. Scott Fitzgerald* (1980).

255   In a 1924 version of the feature, Wilson termed Fitzgerald 'part Irish'. In a 1952 edition, he became 'partly Irish', as discussed in Davis Schlacks, 'F. Scott Fitzgerald, Trickster: Images of Irishness in Edmund Wilson's Bookman Essay', *The F. Scott Fitzgerald Review*, vol. 14, no. 1 (2016), pp. 159–80.

256   *Ibid*.

257   Milford, *Zelda* (1970).

258   FSF to Edmund Wilson, 25 June 1922, in Turnbull, *The Letters of F. Scott Fitzgerald* (1963).

259   '10 Best Books I Have Read', *Jersey City Evening Journal*, 24 April 1923, in Bruccoli, *Some Sort of Epic Grandeur* (2002).

Part 2: Gatsby

The Vegetable

260   FSF to Max Perkins, 'before' 7 November, 1923, in Turnbull, *Scott Fitzgerald* (1962).

261   FSF to Max Perkins, *c.* 12 August 1922, in Bruccoli, *A Life in Letters* (1994).

262     $15,000 for *This Side of Paradise* from Paramount, FSF to Thomas Boyd, March 1923, in Bruccoli, *Correspondence* (1980); $2,500 for *The Beautiful and Damned* from Warner Brothers, FSF to Max Perkins, 21 April 1922, in Bruccoli, *Correspondence* (1980).

263   Meyers, *A Biography* (1994).

264   FSF, 'How to Live on $36,000 a Year', *The Saturday Evening Post*, 5 April 1924.

265   Turnbull, *Scott Fitzgerald* (1962).

266   Mizener, *The Far Side of Paradise* (1965).

267   Zelda Fitzgerald, Summer 1923, Minnesota Historical Society, in Bruccoli, *Some Sort of Epic Grandeur* (2002).

268   FSF Ledger, Transcript, June–July, August 1923, University of South Carolina.

269   FSF, 'A Short Autobiography', *New Yorker*, 25 May 1929.

270   Edmund Wilson to H.L. Mencken, 17 August 1923, in E. Wilson (ed.), *Letters on Literature and Politics, 1912–1972* (Farrar, Straus and Giroux, 2019).

271   FSF Ledger, Transcript, September 1923, University of South Carolina, '… chart out a schedule of work for the rest of the year'; FSF to Holger Lundbergh, 'Summer (?)' 1923, in Bruccoli, *Correspondence* (1980).

272   FSF to Max Perkins, 'before' 7 November, 1923, in Turnbull, *Scott Fitzgerald* (1962).

273   FSF, 'How to Live on $36,000 a Year', *The Saturday Evening Post*, 5
       April 1924.

274   FSF to Thomas Boyd, early 1924, in Bruccoli, *Correspondence*
       (1980).

275   Thomas Boyd to FSF, April 1923, in Bruccoli, *Correspondence*
       (1980).

276   FSF to Max Perkins, summer 1924, in Bruccoli, *A Life in Letters*
       (1994).

277   FSF to Max Perkins, *c.* 10 April 1924, in Bruccoli, *A Life in Letters*
       (1994).

'Absolution'

278   J.L.W. West, *The Great Gatsby F. Scott Fitzgerald*, edited by J.L.W.
       West, III (Cambridge University Press, Cambridge, 2018).

279   The Bowery Boys, 'The Corona Ash Dump: Brooklyn's burden
       on Queens, a vivid literary inspiration and bleak, rat-filled landscape',
       podcast, 9 May 2013.

280   Max Perkins to FSF, 16 April 1924, in Kuehl and Bryer, *Dear Scott,
       Dear Max* (1971).

281   FSF to Max Perkins, *c.* 10 April 1924, in Bruccoli, *A Life in Letters*
       (1994).

282   FSF to John Jamieson, 15 April 1934, in Turnbull, *The Letters*
       (1963).

283   FSF Ledger, Transcript, September 1907, University of South
       Carolina.

284   FSF to John Jamieson, 15 April 1934, in Turnbull, *The Letters*
       (1963).

285   FSF to Max Perkins, 18 June 1924, in Bruccoli, *A Life in Letters*
       (1994).

Exile

286   FSF Ledger, Transcript, January–April 1924, University of South Carolina.

287   FSF to Kenneth Littauer, 29 September 1939, in Bruccoli, *A Life in Letters* (1994).

288   FSF to Thomas Boyd, May 1924, in Bruccoli, *Correspondence* (1980).

289   FSF to Harold Ober, received 10 June 1924, in M. Bruccoli, *As Ever, Scott Fitz: Letters Between F. Scott Fitzgerald and His Literary Agent, Harold Ober, 1919–1940* (Woburn Press, United Kingdom, 1973).

290   FSF to Max Perkins, 18 June 1924, in Bruccoli, *A Life in Letters* (1994).

291   *The Great Gatsby*: 'Father arrived from a town in Minnesota', 'James Gatz of North Dakota'.

292   This line is edited out in later drafts. See J.L.W. West, *Trimalchio: An Early Version of The Great Gatsby*, edited with an Introduction by J.L.W. West III (Charles Scribner's Sons, New York, 2014).

293   FSF to Robert Kerr, June 1924, in Bruccoli, *A Life in Letters* (1994).

Incorruptible Dream

294   FSF and Zelda Fitzgerald, 'Show Mr. and Mrs. F. to Number—', *Esquire*, 1934.

295   FSF to Edmund Wilson, summer 1924, in Bruccoli, *A Life in Letters* (1994).

296   FSF to Thomas Boyd, 23 June 1924, in Bruccoli, *Correspondence* (1980).

Drive to Destruction

297   Mizener, *The Far Side of Paradise* (1965).

298 *NYT*, 'Irish Societies Object to "Queensboro" Instead of Blackwell's Island', 26 September 1908.

Mobsters

299 FSF, 'How to Live on Practically Nothing a Year', 1924.

300 FSF to Thomas Boyd, 23 June 1924, in Bruccoli, *Correspondence* (1980).

301 Bruccoli, *Some Sort of Epic Grandeur* (2002).

302 H.H. Kruse, *F. Scott Fitzgerald at work: The making of 'The Great Gatsby'* (University of Alabama Press, Alabama, 2014).

303 A. Sargeant, 'Meyer Wolfsheim – Arnold Rothstein, Scott Fitzgerald and *The Great Gatsby*', 2022, www.monocledmutineer. co.uk/meyer-wolfsheim-rothstein-fitzgerald-gatsby.

304 *Ibid*.

305 Kruse, *The making of 'The Great Gatsby'* (2014).

306 *Ibid*.

307 *Ibid*.

308 Zelda Fitzgerald, summer 1923, Minnesota Historical Society, quoted in Bruccoli, *Some Sort of Epic Grandeur* (2002).

309 Mizener, *The Far Side of Paradise* (1965).

310 FSF, *My Lost City* (2005).

311 D. Pietrusza, *Rothstein: The Life, Times, and Murder of the Criminal Genius Who Fixed the 1919 World Series* (2nd ed., Basic Books, 2011).

312 Sargeant, 'Meyer Wolfsheim – Arnold Rothstein, Scott Fitzgerald and *The Great Gatsby*', 2022.

313 *Ibid*.

314 Turnbull, *Scott Fitzgerald* (1962).

The Big Crisis

315   FSF to Max Perkins, *c.* 10 July 1924, in Bruccoli, *Correspondence* (1980). Note: Turnbull dated the letter 'circa July 16' which is inconsistent with the 'Big Crisis' of the same date, in Turnbull, *The Letters* (1963).

316   Alexander McKaig's diary, 12 April, 13 June, 12 October, 16 October 1920, in Turnbull, *Scott Fitzgerald* (1962).

317   FSF, *My Lost City* (2005).

318   Z. Fitzgerald, *Save Me the Waltz* (1932).

319   FSF to Edmund Wilson, 15 August 1919, in Bruccoli, *A Life in Letters* (1994).

320   Admiral Edouard Jozan to Nancy Milford, 17 February 1967, in Milford, *Zelda* (1970).

321   FSF to Zelda Fitzgerald, 'Summer?' 1930, in Bruccoli, *A Life in Letters* (1994).

322   Zelda Fitzgerald to FSF, 'Late summer/early fall 1930', in Bruccoli, *A Life in Letters* (1994).

323   FSF to Harold Ober, 7 July 1924, in Bruccoli, *As Ever* (1973).

324   FSF Ledger, Transcript, August 1924, University of South Carolina.

325   FSF, 'Pasting It Together' (1936).

326   FSF to Max Perkins, 27 August 1924, in Bruccoli, *A Life in Letters* (1994).

327   FSF Ledger, Transcript, September 1924, University of South Carolina.

328   FSF Notebooks, no. 839, Bruccoli, *The Notebooks of F. Scott Fitzgerald* (1978).

329   West, *Trimalchio* (2014).

Polite Indifference

330   FSF Notebooks, no. 1610, Bruccoli, *The Notebooks of F. Scott Fitzgerald* (1978).

Repeat the Past

331   FSF to Max Perkins, mid-July 1922, in Bruccoli, *Correspondence* (1980)

332   FSF to Moran Tudury, postmarked 11 April, 1924, in Bruccoli, *Correspondence* (1980).

333   FSF to Ludlow Fowler, August 1924, in Bruccoli, *A Life in Letters* (1994).

334   FSF to Harold Ober, received 12 January 1925, in Bruccoli, *As Ever* (1973).

335   **Fuller and McGee Case**

Bruccoli, *Correspondence* (1980).

336   FSF to Max Perkins, *c*. 24 April 1925, in Bruccoli, *A Life in Letters* (1994).

337   FSF to Harold Ober, 20 September 1924, in Bruccoli, *A Life in Letters* (1994).

338   FSF to Max Perkins, *c*. 10 October 1924, in Kuehl and Bryer, *Dear Scott, Dear Max* (1971).

339   Max Perkins to FSF, 18 October 1924, in Kuehl and Bryer, *Dear Scott, Dear Max* (1971).

340   FSF to Harold Ober, 19 October 1924, in Bruccoli, *As Ever* (1973).

341   FSF to Harold Ober, 25 October 1924, in Bruccoli, *As Ever* (1973).

342   FSF to Max Perkins, 27 October 1924, in Kuehl and Bryer, *Dear Scott, Dear Max* (1971).

343   FSF to Edmund Wilson, July 1921, in Bruccoli, *A Life in Letters* (1994).

344   FSF Ledger, Transcript, September 1924, University of South Carolina.

345   FSF to Max Perkins, *c.* 7 November 1924, in Kuehl and Bryer, *Dear Scott, Dear Max* (1971).

346   Max Perkins to FSF, 14 November 1924, in Kuehl and Bryer, *Dear Scott, Dear Max* (1971).

347   Max Perkins to FSF, 20 November 1924, in Kuehl and Bryer, *Dear Scott, Dear Max* (1971).

348   Mellow, *Invented Lives* (1984).

349   FSF to Max Perkins, *c.* 1 December 1924, in Kuehl and Bryer, *Dear Scott, Dear Max* (1971).

350   FSF to Harold Ober, received 26 November 1924, in Bruccoli, *As Ever* (1973).

351   FSF to Max Perkins, *c.* 1 December 1924, in Kuehl and Bryer, *Dear Scott, Dear Max* (1971).

352   Max Perkins to FSF, 16 December 1924, in Kuehl and Bryer, *Dear Scott, Dear Max* (1971); Notes from FSF to Max Perkins, *c.* 20 December 1924, in Kuehl and Bryer, *Dear Scott, Dear Max* (1971).

353   FSF to Max Perkins, *c.* 20 December 1924, in Kuehl and Bryer, *Dear Scott, Dear Max* (1971).

354   Max Perkins to FSF, 19 December 1924, in Kuehl and Bryer, *Dear Scott, Dear Max* (1971).

355   FSF to Max Perkins, *c.* 20 December 1924, in Kuehl and Bryer, *Dear Scott, Dear Max* (1971).

356   *NYT*, 19 July 1923.

357   *NYT*, 28 July 1923; 'A Jazz Age Autopsy', *Vanity Fair*, May 2005.

358   *NYT*, 21 August 1923.

359   *NYT*, 8 October 1932.

360   West, *Trimalchio* (2014).

361   FSF to Harold Ober, 22 December 1924, in Bruccoli, *As Ever* (1973).

362   FSF to Thomas Boyd, 'Late 1924 (?)', in Bruccoli, *Correspondence* (1980).

363   FSF to Harold Ober, received 23 January 1925, in Bruccoli, *As Ever* (1973).

Plaza Scene

364   FSF to Harold Ober, received 12 January 1925, in Bruccoli, *As Ever* (1973).

365   FSF Ledger, Transcript, November 1924, University of South Carolina.

366   FSF to Zelda Fitzgerald, 'Summer? 1930', in Bruccoli, *A Life in Letters* (1994).

367   FSF to Max Perkins, *c.* 15 January 1925, in Kuehl and Bryer, *Dear Scott, Dear Max* (1971).

368   FSF to Max Perkins, 24 January 1925, in Kuehl and Bryer, *Dear Scott, Dear Max* (1971).

369   FSF to Max Perkins, *c.* 20 December 1924, in Bruccoli, *A Life in Letters* (1994).

370   FSF to Harold Ober, received 22 December 1924, in Bruccoli, *As Ever* (1973).

371   FSF to Max Perkins, Late January 1925, in Bruccoli, *Correspondence* (1980).

372   FSF to Harold Ober, received 5 February 1925, in Bruccoli, *As Ever* (1973).

373   FSF to Max Perkins, 18 February 1925, in Mizener, *The Far Side of Paradise* (1965).

374   Galley 40, The Great Gatsby – Trimalchio Galleys, Princeton University Library (hereafter PUL).

375   FSF to Max Perkins, 18 February 1925, in Kuehl and Bryer, *Dear Scott, Dear Max* (1971).

376   Max Perkins to FSF, 19 March 1920, in Kuehl and Bryer, *Dear Scott, Dear Max* (1971).

377   FSF to Max Perkins, *c.* 10 July 1925, in Bruccoli, *A Life in Letters* (1994).

Death of an Irishman

378   Galley 45, The Great Gatsby – Trimalchio Galleys, PUL.

379   FSF to John Peale Bishop, *c.* 9 August 1925, in Bruccoli, *A Life in Letters* (1994).

380   'Found in the Vault: An Inscription From F. Scott Fitzgerald', 17 December 2013, Provenance Project, Michigan State University Special Collections Library.

381   John O'Hara to Gerald Murphy, 30 July 1962, in Mellow, *Invented lives* (1984).

382   Laura Hearne, 'A Summer with Scott Fitzgerald', *Esquire*, December 1964.

383   Sara Murphy to FSF, *c.* 1934, in Bruccoli, *Correspondence* (1980).

384   Ernest Hemingway to Max Perkins, 30 April 1934, in M.J. Bruccoli, *The Only Thing that Counts: The Ernest Hemingway/Maxwell Perkins Correspondence, 1925–1947* (Scribner, New York, 1996).

385   FSF to John Peale Bishop, August 1925, in Bruccoli, *Correspondence* (1980).

Confession of Being a Gael

386   FSF to Ober, received 5 March 1925, in Bruccoli, *As Ever* (1973).

387   FSF to Perkins, cable 19 March 1925, quotation marks were added by Perkins on receipt, in Bruccoli, *Correspondence* (1980).

388   FSF to Max Perkins, 10 April 1925, in Kuehl and Bryer, *Dear Scott, Dear Max* (1971).

389   See FSF to Ober, received 13 April 1925, in Bruccoli, *As Ever*
       (1973).

390   FSF to Ober, received 13 April 1925, in Bruccoli, *As Ever* (1973).

391   Max Perkins to FSF, 20 April 1925, in Bruccoli, *Correspondence*
       (1980).

392   FSF to Max Perkins, *c.* 24 April 1925, in Kuehl and Bryer, *Dear
       Scott, Dear Max* (1971).

393   Max Perkins to FSF, 25 April 1925, in Kuehl and Bryer, *Dear Scott,
       Dear Max* (1971).

394   Rodger L. Tarr, *As Ever Yours: The Letters of Max Perkins and
       Elizabeth Lemmon* (Penn State University Press, 2003).

395   FSF to Max Perkins, *c.* 22 May, in Kuehl and Bryer, *Dear Scott,
       Dear Max* (1971).

396   FSF to Max Perkins, *c.* 22 May, in Kuehl and Bryer, *Dear Scott,
       Dear Max* (1971).

397   FSF to Zelda Fitzgerald, 'Summer? 1930', in Bruccoli, *A Life in
       Letters* (1994).

398   FSF to Max Perkins, *c.* 10 September 1925, in Kuehl and Bryer,
       Dear Scott, Dear Max (1971).

399   James L.W. West and Anne Margaret Daniel (eds), *The Great
       Gatsby: The 1926 Broadway Script* (Cambridge University Press,
       Cambridge, 2024).

400   Zelda Fitzgerald to Scottie, 1927, PUL, in Mellow, *Invented lives*
       (1984).

401   FSF to Zelda Fitzgerald, 'Summer? 1930', in Bruccoli, *A Life in
       Letters* (1994).

402   Donaldson, *Fool for Love* (2012).

403   FSF, 'Pasting It Together' (1936).

404   Scott Donaldson, *Hemingway vs. Fitzgerald: The Rise and Fall of a
       Literary Friendship* (The Overlook Press, New York, 1999).

405   Ernest Hemingway to Max Perkins, 23 February 1933, in Bruccoli, *The Only Thing that Counts* (1996).

406   FSF to John O'Hara, 18 July 1933, in Bruccoli, *A Life in Letters* (1994).

407   FSF, 'More Than Just a House', *Saturday Evening Post*, 24 June 1933.

408   Charles Fanning, *The Irish Voice in America: 250 years of Irish-American fiction* (University Press of Kentucky, 2000).

Body of an American

409   Bruccoli, *Some Sort of Epic Grandeur* (2002).

410   Charles McGrath, 'Fitzgerald as Screenwriter: No Hollywood Ending', *NYT*, 22 April 2004.

411   *Ibid*.

412   Sheilah Graham, *Beloved Infidel: The Education of a Woman* (Holt, New York, 1958).

413   M.J. Bruccoli, *Selected letters of John O'Hara* (Random House, 1978).

414   The story had been reported to Arthur Mizener as coming from Alan Campbell, who was then Dorothy Parker's husband (Mizener, *The Far Side of Paradise* (1965)).

415   FSF Notebooks, nos 1238, 1192, 346, Bruccoli, *The Notebooks of F. Scott Fitzgerald* (1978).

416   FSF to Lois Moran, 8 March 1935, in Bruccoli, *Correspondence* (1980).

417   'That Sad Young Man', *The New Yorker*, 17 April 1926.

418   FSF Notebooks, no. 598, Bruccoli, *The Notebooks of F. Scott Fitzgerald* (1978).

419   FSF Notebooks, no. 2037, Bruccoli, *The Notebooks of F. Scott Fitzgerald* (1978).

Appendix

De Valera in America

420   *NYT*, 22 June 1919, p. 12.

421   'Statement of Edward F. McSweeney' (undated typescript, responding to an attack by McCartan in the *New York World*, 22 June 1920), Cohalan Papers, 10/13, quoted in D. Fitzpatrick, *Harry Boland's Irish Revolution* (Cork University Press, Cork, 2003), p. 144.

422   D. McCullagh, *De Valera: Rise (1882–1932)* (vol. 1, Gill Books, Dublin, 2017) , 30/3/20, EDV diary for 1920, P150/264.

423   McGuire to Boland, 16 November 1920, in J. Fahey, *James K. McGuire: Boy Mayor and Irish Nationalist* (Syracuse University Press, Syracuse, 2014).

424   McCartan to McGarrity, 12 July 1920, McGarrity Papers, National Library, MS 17457/13, quoted in Fitzpatrick, *Harry Boland's Irish Revolution* (2003), p. 189; Seán, Cronin, *The McGarrity Papers* (Anvil Books, Tralee, 1972), p. 83.

425   O'Mara to de Valera, 25 April 1921, P. in Lavelle, *James O'Mara: The Story of an Original Sinn Féiner* (Clonmore & Reynolds, Dublin, 2011), p. 245.

426   Devoy to McCartan, 21 April 1919, in Lynch, *History of the Friends of Irish Freedom* (1930–39).

427   *GA*, 20 September 1924, p. 2.

428   *IP*, editorial, 1 November 1919, p. 4.

429   Minutes, in Lynch, *History of the Friends of Irish Freedom* (1930–39).

430   Devoy to McCartan, 21 April 1919, in Lynch, *History of the Friends of Irish Freedom* (1930–39).